THE

EVERYTHING KIDS'®

TRAVEL ACTIVITY BOOK

Games to play, songs to sing, fun stuff to do—
guaranteed to keep you busy the whole ride!

Erik A. Hanson and Jeanne K. Hanson

Adams Media Corporation
Avon, Massachusetts

EDITORIAL
Publishing Director: Gary M. Krebs
Managing Editor: Kate McBride
Copy Chief: Laura MacLaughlin
Acquisitions Editor: Cheryl Kimball
Development Editor: Christel A. Shea

PRODUCTION
Production Director: Susan Beale
Production Manager: Michelle Roy Kelly
Series Designer: Colleen Cunningham
Layout and Graphics: Arlene Apone,
Paul Beatrice, Brooke Camfield,
Colleen Cunningham, Daria Perreault,
Frank Rivera

An Everything® Series Book.
Everything® and everything.com® are registered trademarks of F+W Media, Inc.

Published by Adams Media, a division of F+W Media, Inc.
57 Littlefield Street, Avon, MA 02322. U.S.A.
www.adamsmedia.com

ISBN 13: 978-1-58062-641-5
ISBN 10: 1-58062-641-6
Printed by RR Donnelley, Harrisonburg, VA, USA
July 2016

20 19 18 17 16 15

Library of Congress Cataloging-in-Publication Data

Hanson, Erik A.
    The everything kids' travel activity book / by Erik A. Hanson and Jeanne K.
Hanson.
        p.   cm.
    Summary: Presents observation games, rhyming games, and other activities
to play during every mile of the trip, even during bathroom time.
    ISBN 1-58062-641-6
    1. Games for travelers—Juvenile literature. 2. Family recreation—Juvenile
literature. [1. Games for travelers. 2. Games. 3. Family recreation.] I.
Hanson, Jeanne K. II. Title
GV1206 H35 2002
793.7—dc21   2001055307

Cover illustrations by Dana Regan.
Interior illustrations by Kurt Dolber with additional illustrations by Kathie Kelleher and Barry Littmann.
Puzzles by Beth Blair.

Puzzle Power Software by Centron Software Technologies, Inc. was used to create puzzle grids.

This book is available at quantity discounts for bulk purchases.
For information, call 1-800-289-0963.

See the entire Everything® series at *everything.com*.

Contents

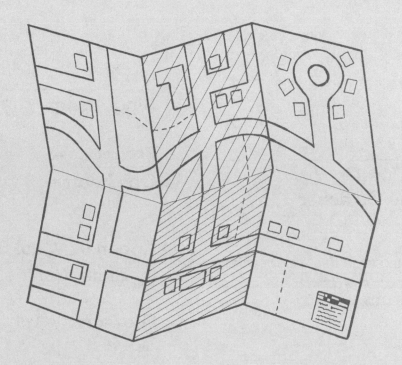

This book belongs to: _____

Dates of travel: _____

Travel destination: _____

Introduction

This book is going to be fun—and you'll learn stuff, too. It will also keep you busy so you won't be tempted to fight with your brother or sister, or kick the back of anybody's seat. It will also prevent whining (unless you're getting really hungry). One warning: this book will not keep you from having to stop at the gas station to go to the bathroom!

So grab your gear and get ready to hit the road!

Know Before You Go

Print out the Web site (or part of it) for the place you're visiting. If you're traveling through the United States, or traveling in another country, go to the sites for every city you'll visit. You can learn a lot about the things to do there, and what there is to see. Take the printouts on your trip and teach stuff to your parents!

Down Memory Lane

Ask your parent(s) to tell you about family vacations they took when they were kids. Were they quiet in the car, or did they keep asking, "Are we there yet?" Did your grandparents make them stop every two hours to go to the bathroom?

Then find out, too, of course, what wonderful things they saw. And what really surprised them about a trip. Do they take you to some of the places they used to visit? Ask them what's the same and what has changed.

Word Search

In this word grid, see if you can find fifteen things you might spot when driving along the highway. The words can go backwards, forwards, up, down, and diagonally.

BILLBOARD
CONSTRUCTION
EXIT SIGN
GUARDRAIL
MILE MARKER
MOTELS
POLICE CAR
REST AREA
ROUTE NUMBER
RV
SKIDS
TOLLBOOTH
TOUR BUS
TRUCK
TRUCK STOP

```
M I L E M A R K E R M O R
E T R E X I T S I G N C H
A T N E T W O M I L O A L
R R L I B O N M T N I E I
A U L E S M O O S K F R A
C C P A V E U T D C R A R
E K O A D R R N S U I T D
C S N T B U S H E R I S R
I T S U C L C O V T U E A
L O S T E N T E Y A U R U
O P I T L S K I D S O O G
P O O H T O O B L L O T R
N M N E D R A O B L L I B
```

Extra puzzle points: After you have circled all the listed words, read the leftover letters from left to right, and top to bottom. You will find a fast fact about how many miles of paved roads there are in the world.

What to Pack for Food

Of course, you could stuff yourself with gas station candy bars all day, but you'd turn into a sugar zombie or something.

Instead, take along some snacks that are better for you, and not very messy. These goodies don't get instantly rotten or smashed too easily:

- Small boxes of raisins
- Foil packages of cherry tomatoes
- Salt-free peanuts, cashews, or almonds, in a tin
- Carrot and celery sticks
- Wrapped burritos (with no meat to spoil)
- Orange slices (peel the oranges and separate the sections before you leave home)
- Grapes

The fruits and vegetables naturally have a lot of water in them, so they'll quench your thirst, too.

What to Pack for Fun

You don't need to go out and buy a lot of stuff, but look for which of these things you have already at home. Dump them in your own backpack with your name on it in big letters. That way you can share when you want to, and you'll know what things are yours when it's time to put them away.

Put in there:

- An Etch-A-Sketch (try the pocket size)
- Travel Scrabble or Boggle (with magnetic letters)
- Two dice
- A drawing pad and some magic markers with caps that stay on
- Colored pencils
- Tape, safety scissors
- Mad Libs, magazines
- Audiotapes or compact discs, or maybe your own mix of songs you all know so everyone can sing along
- A laptop computer, if you have one

Postcard Art Collage

For a fun activity, make a collage of postcards or pieces of postcards you buy on your trip. (If you want to actually *keep* the postcard—and you want it on your collage—buy two, if that's not too expensive.)

Get a piece of cardboard (like the back of a candy bar box from the local convenience store), and also some tape and a pair of safety scissors. (It's important to use safety scissors so no one gets cut or hurt if there is a sharp turn, big bump, or other sudden movement.)

Make a big outdoor scene by taping together similar postcards or connecting the horizons on different postcards. Or join some pieces of postcards together to form the shape of a mountain or something you've seen in the area.

MPG

The letters "MPG" are an acronym (an abbreviation using the first letters) for "Miles Per Gallon." Figure out what this acronym stands for by looking at the picture.

SWAK

Web Sites

It's a good idea to find out about the places you'll visit. Sometimes, other sites will tell you what to do while you are traveling and when you get there.

A good Web site to go to before you leave is Family.com, one of Disney Online's Web sites. You can search for information about a specific city or state—and get a list of the best places to go for fun. You can also look at the site's "Travel Checklists." They give you information on what to pack for certain kinds of vacations, such as ones at the beach or in the mountains.

For the Whole Trip

Why not keep track of the miles you travel on this trip?

If you are taking a train or an airplane, talk to the conductor or one of the flight attendants. They will be able to tell you (or find out) how long your trip is.

If you're driving, ask your parents to tell you the mileage at the beginning and end of every day. Subtract the beginning number from the end number to get a day's total, and record them here:

Miles on Day One: _____   Miles on Day Three: _____

Miles on Day Two: _____   Miles on Day Four: _____
(and so on)

Add up the grand, exhausting total, and put
it here: _____.

Wow!

Traveler: Is this the bus to California?

Ticket Agent: Yes, it goes to California in ten minutes.

Traveler: Wow! That's a fast trip!

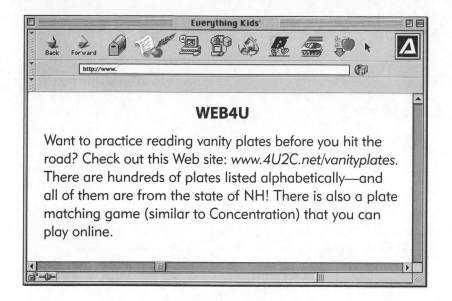

WEB4U

Want to practice reading vanity plates before you hit the road? Check out this Web site: *www.4U2C.net/vanityplates*. There are hundreds of plates listed alphabetically—and all of them are from the state of NH! There is also a plate matching game (similar to Concentration) that you can play online.

FUN FACT

History of the Car

The automobile was invented about 1890, but almost no one had a car until Henry Ford invented the Model T. Ford and his factory built the cars on an assembly line, a process that made everything faster. His company built 15 million Model T cars between 1908 and 1928.

To start early-model cars, you had to turn a crank, which made the spark that started the engine. Luckily for us, the cranks were eventually replaced with the modern car battery.

Another good Web site to consult for travel information is the About.com site "Travel with Kids." You can find links to other Web sites with very detailed information about specific places—and About.com has links within the site to "Fun Places" to go and "Travel Games" to play in the car.

Chapter 1

Count the Cows? Yes, and the Ostriches . . .

MPG

The letters "MPG" are an acronym (an abbreviation using the first letters) for "Miles Per Gallon." Figure out what this acronym stands for by looking at the picture.

Today's special is a tomato sandwich.

Put bacon and lettuce on mine.

BLT

Fun counting games will keep you busy for as long as you want to play them. And even if the people you are traveling with stop playing, you can continue the game on your own. You can count red cars, train stations, or your brother's snorts—whatever you can think of. You can count something you seem to see on every corner, or maybe something completely new will catch your eye. If you're driving through Alaska, you might want to count snow-topped mountains, or even seals in the harbors. If you're in the Florida Keys, it might be pelicans or bridges. Be creative and have fun! By the end of the whole trip, you could even go back and see who won the most games.

Gas Station Count

Count all the gas stations you pass this morning before lunch. Remember to include unusual types of gas stations, such as "Fina," and various kinds of truck stops. Have one person on each side of the car look out his or her own side for a while. If you don't see very many, ask yourself why that is. Does the area just not have very many people living in it? Is the highway you're on not a major route for trucks? Maybe there isn't a good explanation. But you can still think about these kinds of things.

Yes, Count the Cows

Between lunch and the next bathroom stop, count up every cow you see! If you're in a city, you might not see cows, but maybe police on horseback.

What's in a Tree?

Count all the different types of trees you see out the window while you're stopped for lunch or dinner. Unless you're an expert in **botany**, you probably won't know what the different names are, but you can still notice the number of different types. If you see a "forest" with trees that are very, very evenly spaced, it's probably a planted or "planned" forest. Those trees may have been planted there to block the wind, make a house more private, or to sell later for lumber. If you have a tree guide from a library or bookstore, you can try to identify different specific trees. Note the **latitude** that you're driving at and see if the tree is native to the region you're in.

Cars Are Colorful

Shout out when you see the colors of a rainbow! Who is the first one to see a purple car? Next, in order, look for a blue car, then green, yellow, orange, and, last, red. Make sure you all understand the rules: trucks and buses don't count. If you are the first to see a real rainbow, then you've won, hands down. So you can keep track of how far along you are, circle each color word in this paragraph as you see the matching car.

WORDS to KNOW

botany: The science and study of plants and plant life. If you study botany, you'll learn why apple trees grow in the north, orange trees grow in the south, and cacti grow in the desert.

latitude: A number that tells you where you are between the equator (latitude 0°) and either the North or South poles (latitude 90°). For example, Minneapolis, Minnesota, is at 45° latitude, exactly halfway between the equator and the North Pole.

Pickup Truck

Start at the letter B marked with the white dot. Follow the truck clockwise around the wheel picking up every third letter. Write them on the lines below. When you have finished, you will find the answer to this riddle: Why are sleepy people like automobile wheels?

Why are sleepy people like automobile wheels?

_ _ _ _ _ _

_ _ _ _

_ _ _ _

_ _ _ _ _!

Passing on the Left

If you're driving on a two-lane road, count the number of cars your car passes in an hour. A lot of people drive somewhat oddly on highways. Some will drive just below the speed limit for no good reason. Others will drive fast enough and then slow down without any reason. Others will drive way over the speed limit. A driver who doesn't keep up with the overall traffic's speed can actually create more danger by going too slowly. And, of course, driving too fast can get you into a big wreck!

Uhh, What?

Don't tell them ahead of time, but count the number of times people with you say "uh." Just a half an hour will probably get you a pretty high total!

Junk Food Bites

How many bites of junk food has your brother or sister snarfed down this afternoon? If you're not sure what counts as a "junk," ask your parents.

Funny Business

How many businesses will you drive past today that have funny names? Start looking for ones like "Earl's Pearls" or "The Dew Drop Inn." You could even make a list for your whole trip.

If you were to start your own business, what kind would it be? One of the things that helps a business is having a clever and unique name—that way, people will remember it. Maybe the signs and businesses you see on your trip will help you with ideas of your own.

How did one road greet another road?

Hi, way!

Your Car's Name Is Special

Count the number of words you can make out of the letters in your car's name. For example, if you have a Nissan, you'd probably start with "is," "an," and "nan." Do the same thing for each of the names of the people in your family.

Snort

Count the number of times your brothers, sisters, or friends sneeze, cough, and sniffle in one hour this morning. Are they gross or what?

A Short Trip

Most people travel from where they live and work to a vacation spot so they can relax. Can you get from "TRAVEL" to "RELAX" in just four steps?

TRAVEL

1. _____

2. _____

3. _____

4. RELAX_____

In each step you can do only one of three things: omit a letter, switch two letters with each other, or change one letter into another letter. Write your changes step by step on the lines provided.

What Is a Cough?

Coughing is our bodies' way to get something irritating out of our **respiratory** systems.

A cough begins in the lungs (we have two of them). Powerful muscles around the lungs contract, then expand, pushing out the air and mucus. Our vocal cords automatically close partway, moving aside a little to let the cough out. (This is why you can't talk while you're coughing.)

Each cough is a real windstorm—people cough out air (and mucus) at the rate of about 300 mph. This is faster than a lot of hurricanes!

WORDS to KNOW

respiratory: Having to do with the body's breathing system.

Miles per Gallon Math

When you stop to buy gas, fill the tank, and ask the driver to reset the lower odometer (the tripometer) to zero right at the gas station.

The next time you stop for gas, check the tripometer to see how many miles you have gone. Fill the tank again, and write down the number on the pump's gauge. That will tell you how much gas you have used since the last fill-up. Now you're ready for some real math!

Divide the number of miles on the tripometer by the number of gallons of gas you have used. The result is the miles per gallon! If the number you get is especially high or especially low, that might just mean that you've been driving in the country with few stops or slow-downs (which gives really high gas mileage), or all in a city (this gives really low gas mileage). Probably, you'll be somewhere in between.

Higher Math, with Paper

Make a graph of how your speed changes once you leave the highway. Choose a time when you're not on a straight freeway, and ask your parent, or whoever is driving the car, if he or she can help you. (You don't want to distract anyone who is trying to follow directions, or drive around a strange city.) For five minutes, ask the driver to tell you the speed of your car every thirty seconds (by your watch). Then make a little graph to show how the speed changes. Do this by drawing a little ladder, with a higher rung for every ten miles per hour faster. Put a dot for each speed.

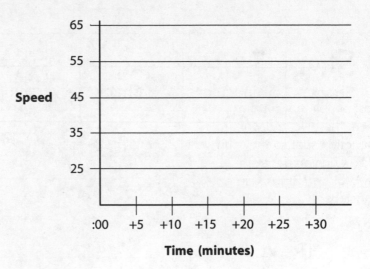

Potty Stop

Count the number of times anyone and everyone you're traveling with has to stop for the bathroom today. Sometimes, it's nice when someone else has to call for the pit stop—then it's not always you! If you're on an airplane or train, always say "excuse me" if you need to climb past people to get to the bathroom. Usually, they'll stand up to let you out.

Let's Get Packing

In the space next to the word box (or on a separate piece of paper) list all the words in the boxes with the number 1. Then do the same for the words in the boxes numbered 2, 3, 4, 5, and 6. Finally, write each list of words as a sentence to find out what Kayla and Dustin had to do to get ready for their hiking trip.

1 Call	**4** and	**2** bug	**1** to	**5** extra	**2** block
4 bottles,	**1** Kelly	**5** and	**3** flashlight	**6** Find	**4** snacks,
2 Buy	**5** Pack	**6** bird	**4** water	**1** directions	**2** spray.
3 the	**4** Fill	**1** for	**6** and	**5** ponchos	**6** books.
1 Short	**6** binoculars	**3** Check	**2** sun	**3** batteries.	**2** and
4 chocolate!	**1** park.	**4** make	**5** socks.	**1** State	**4** get

1. _____

2. _____

3. _____

4. _____

5. _____

6. _____

WORDS to KNOW

rural: Relating to open spaces, as in the country. Rural areas are usually very far from cities. The houses are usually far apart, and you may see a lot of farms.

populated: Refers to the number of people in an area. Cities are heavily populated, which means that many people live and work there. Do you think rural areas are heavily populated?

What kind of egg travels to faraway places?

An egg-splorer!

Billboard Alert

All afternoon, count the number of billboards you see. Pay attention to how they change as you go from area to area. How are city billboards different from **rural** ones?

The Wild Ones

Count the number of wild animals, of any kind, that you see—or that you smell. (Maybe a skunk??) If you're traveling in the morning through quiet and wooded areas, you might see a deer. And trains usually go through less **populated** areas where there are more wild animals. You have to pay attention, though, because animals in the wild are experts at keeping themselves hidden!

Hitchhikers

Count the number of hitchhikers, if any, that you pass on the road today. Ask your parents why there are—or aren't—many of them around here today. Have you ever driven near a prison and seen a sign that says, "Prison Area—DO NOT Pick up Hitchhikers"? These warnings are for real!

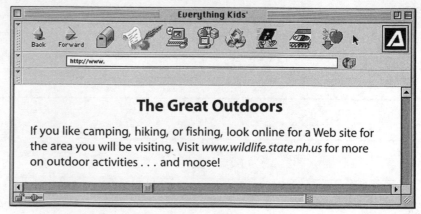

The Great Outdoors

If you like camping, hiking, or fishing, look online for a Web site for the area you will be visiting. Visit *www.wildlife.state.nh.us* for more on outdoor activities . . . and moose!

The First Billboards

Once upon a time, there were no billboards! They first began to "sprout up" along highways when more and more people started taking car trips in the 1940s and 1950s.

The very first billboards were called "Burma Shave Signs" because they all advertised the same shaving cream, called Burma Shave. Every sign was red and white, and displayed a line of a poem. They were small, only about two or three feet long and two or three feet wide. The billboards usually came in groups of five signs. The signs were maybe twenty yards apart or so, in a line along the side of the highway. Almost none of these poems had anything to do with shaving cream, and none had pictures. But people thought billboards were clever and very cool!

Here is an example: "He who drives" (printed on the first sign), "While he's been drinking" (on the second sign), "Depends on you" (on the third sign), "To do his thinking" (on the fourth sign) "—Burma Shave" (on the fifth sign). Get it?

 A billboard designer thinks about questions like these: How can I get a person who's driving or walking by to notice the billboard for my product? What makes a billboard stand out? You can answer these questions—after all, you are a consumer, someone who has bought things.

Maybe you already created a new product with a catchy name. Think of a cool slogan for the product, or come up with an image or scene that would sell it without using any words. Think about the size and colors of your letters and words. Remember that if you want to sell something with a billboard, you'll have to grab people's attention in a split second.

Draw a billboard for a product you like

Design a License Plate

You may have noticed that states sometimes change the designs of their license plates. A state may also change the "slogan" or words on its license plate.

Come up with your own slogans and designs for different states' license plates. When picking slogans, you can either be serious or goofy! The same goes for the design. On real license plates, often the colors will have something to do with the state's geography or its famous places, like green for a state that's known for all its forests. But this doesn't have to be true. You could draw a joke license plate with a picture of the motel you stayed at and a slogan like "The rain-soaked state," if it was raining while you were there.

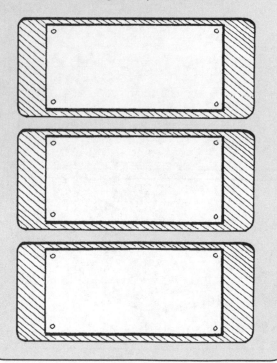

License Plate Delight

When you're in the middle of a state, any state, choose half an hour in which you count the number of license plates from the state you are in *and* the number of plates you see from all the other states in the country, combined. How do you think the numbers will change when you are near the border of a state? What are the results when you try in a city?

Sunny Day Alert

This morning, at your lunch stop, and in the afternoon when you stop for gas, ask your parent or sibling to measure the length of your shadow on the ground. If you don't have a ruler, you can measure it just by having the person "walk measure" it by going toe to heel. Maybe you'll be only "two mom feet" at two in the afternoon, but six at suppertime. What happens when you measure yourself at noon?

In the early morning and late afternoon, the sun is closer to the horizon, so it casts long shadows. During the middle of the day, when the sun is high in the sky, you'll notice that the shadows are much shorter.

State Your Name

Start this puzzle by unscrambling the names of the following twelve states. Then, use the "nicknames" to figure which states will fit into the grid provided. Remember, not all of the state names will be used! We left some A-M-E-R-I-C-A to help you out!

WEDLAAER

IOLRAFNCAI

FAIRDLO

DINOALERDHS

UTDSOAHTAOK

ZANIROA

MAAABLA

WIAIHA

NOTEVRM

SLAAAK

YCEKKUTN

ICMNIHGA

Golden State

Great Lake State → M   C   A

Green Mountain State

First State

Sunshine State →   R   A   E

I   Aloha State   Grand Canyon State   R   E

Mt. Rushmore State →   A   A

R   A   I

I

A   I   E

A

The Last Frontier

Flattened Animal Alert

All afternoon, count the number of dead animals you see by the side of the road or on the road. It's always sad when an animal gets hit by a car. But did you know that a larger animal, such as a deer or a moose, can total (completely destroy, beyond any chance of repair) the car that hits it? When you see yellow caution signs for deer crossing, pay attention—running into one of those biggies can even kill the people in the car!

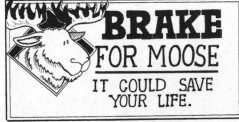

BRAKE FOR MOOSE
IT COULD SAVE YOUR LIFE.

Barnyard Oddities

All day, count up the unusual barnyard critters you see, like **emus**, ostriches, and such. These unusual farms can be in any farming area. Some farmers really do raise these for meat, oil, and hide, instead of the pigs and cows that we're used to. Raising emus in North America started in Texas in 1984, and Canada in 1988—that's not very long ago!

Mileage Math

When you pass the next road sign that gives the distance to the next city in miles, write it down. Then try to figure out how far that is in kilometers. Do you know why people who grew up in most other countries think that the metric system is so much better than the so-called "English" units of measure? (Hint: It has to do with the number 10.)

emu: A flightless bird, related to (but smaller than) the ostrich. Like ostriches, emus are originally from Australia.

Lunchtime, Yet?

According to recent statistics, guess how many pounds of food per year are consumed by the average American? It's 1,425 pounds!

Chapter 2

Round-the-Family
and
Rhyming Games

FUN FACT

What Is Gasoline Made Of?

The gas that makes your car go is mostly oil. This oil is actually the **decomposed** bodies of dead plants and dead animals!

How squished down and how dead? These things died millions of years ago. And their bodies have been smashed under mountains, thick layers of dirt, even the ocean's floor. Thousands of feet squished down. That's why it takes a big drill to drill down deep for oil.

And that's why gasoline is called a "fossil fuel." It's really made of squished up fossils!

WORDS to KNOW

decomposed: Broken down to the most basic parts or elements. Fruits and vegetables that have started to rot are just beginning to decompose.

When you're traveling by car, sometimes you want to do quiet things like listen to your headphones, or do puzzles. But other times, you need a little more excitement. These games get the whole family involved—even the driver can play. And you might be surprised to learn how competitive you really are!

The person who picks the game gets to start the round. Since this is your book, you get first choice! Explain the category to the players, then go around your group until everyone has run out of answers. The last person to have an answer gets to choose the next game.

Round It Up

Birds Around the Family

Have each person name a bird until no one can think of one that hasn't been said. You can decide whether to set a time limit for a person to come up with one. Use your judgment. Obviously a player can't take more than a minute to think of "blue jay" or something easy. As the game goes on, though, you may want to allow a little more time to think of really rare birds.

Doggies

Go around the family thinking of names of dog breeds until you give up with a "woof."

Trashmobile

These kids have been in the back seat too long—look at all the stuff they have piled around them! See if you can find the following sixteen items hidden in the mess.

Snake
Postage stamp
Jack-o-lantern
Sailboat
Toothbrush
Needle
Teapot
Scissors

Fish
Capital letter F
Diamond ring
Key
Dog's head
Pencil
Two slices of
   pizza

Famous Initials

In this game, each person has to come up with the name of a famous person whose last name starts with a certain letter. As a group, you can decide whether the people need to be real people, or if famous names of fictional people count, too. For example, if you are trying to come up with famous people whose last names begin with "P," you'd say "Regis Philbin," and the next person might say "Harry Potter."

Artist on Board

Have each person say a different word to describe a shade of a color. For example—shades of red. The first person says "fire engine red," the next person says "brick," the next person says "scarlet," and so on.

Word Search

In this word grid, see if you can find sixteen things you might spot when driving through a big city. The words can go backwards, forwards, up, down, and diagonally.

BUS STOP
CITY BUS
COFFEE SHOP
CROSSWALK
CROWDS
DINER
HOTDOG CART
MALL

MUSEUM
NEON SIGN
PHONEBOOTH
POLICE
RESTAURANT
SKYSCRAPER
STREETLIGHT
TAXI

```
P D C R O S S W A L K S M
R O I T O K Y O J A T U R
E P H N A M A L L R S N E
S S N S E H A S E E E P P
T U O I E R V E U O E O A
A B R X T E T M N W E L R
U Y N A T L F S Y S I I C
R T X T I M I F D I L C S
A I L G I G O N O W P E Y
N C H E N O P L E C O I K
T T N I P O T S S U B R S
P H O N E B O O T H T W C
O W ☺ T R A C G O D T O H
```

Extra puzzle points: After you have circled all the listed words, read the leftover letters from left to right, and top to bottom. You will find a fast fact about the world's largest city!

School Supplies 101

Name stuff that you would use for school supplies. Think of big things that you need or use (like a desk), as well as small, common items (like pens and pencils). When you start to get stuck, think of what you carry in your book bag, or what your teacher might have on his or her desk.

Be a Plant Scientist

 As you drive through various parts of the country, you'll probably notice some nice flowers, weird rocks, odd shells, colored leaves, and more. A lot of science like this can be explored even in the weeds by the gas station. And more alongside the freeway. Much, much, more on a nice hike in a national park.

Find a box to collect some of the more interesting objects you find. If you don't have a shoe box or something in the car, ask at the gas station for one of those boxes that the candy bars come in. They'll let you have it for free.

Label each "natural treasure" by taping a little note to it. The note might say "this is an elm leaf" or "granite rock." (But you might need to figure that out when you get home.) Or it might just say where you found it ("Florida freeway near Orlando," for example) and on what date. That will help you and your parents or teacher identify it better when you get home—and make it a nice souvenir.

If you find that you have a lot of rocks, you are a geologist. If you chose a lot of flowers, you are a botanist. And if you chose stalks of wild rye (it looks like a fox tail), call yourself an agronomist. Probably you're a little of all of these scientists. Every scientist in the world started by being observant and curious about everyday things.

Science and Measuring in Turn

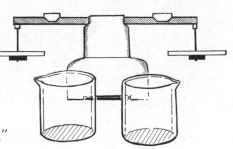

This is a hard game! Keep coming up with scientific rules until you run out of ideas. For example, the starting player might say, "/the speed of light is 186 thousand miles per second." The second one might say, "there are two pints in a quart." The next person says, "the sun is 93 million miles away." The littlest family member can chime in with something like "there are seven days in a week." And so on.

Cars: Name It Time

Come up with the names of car "brands." You don't have to bother with details such as which company is part of which other company. (But that might be another game, if you know enough of the answers to keep it going.) For the first round, anyway, try to keep it simple. One person says "Lexus." The next person says "Ford." Then "Nissan." If you really, really like cars, you can also name different car models, such as Ford's Taurus, Tempo, and Contour.

Everything Kids'

http://www.

Internet Access While You're on Your Trip

You may not have a laptop computer along—most people wouldn't. But it's not that hard to find Web access while on the road. The public libraries in most towns and cities have free access. Stores like Kinko's have computers that you can pay to use. And some places have Internet Cafes where you can pay to go online, too.

FUN FACT

What Makes It Summer?

The sun feels stronger in summer. Why? Some people think that the sun is closer to the Earth in the summer—but it is not. The sun is actually no closer to our planet in January than it is in July. What makes summer is the angle, the slant, of the earth facing the sun.

The Northern Hemisphere (the northern half of our planet above the equator) is toward the sun between April and November. Remember that when it's summer for us, it's winter for all the people in the Southern Hemisphere—South America and Africa and so on. We're getting the high angle when they get the shallow angle. And vice versa.

FUN FACT

Don't Choke On Those Raisins!

Why do people choke? We choke when something takes the wrong "road." At the back of the throat are two choices for stuff to go down: One "road" leads down your **trachea.** The other leads down your **esophagus,** then on to your stomach.

If you're surprised, or just distracted, you may send some spit down the trachea instead of down the esophagus. If you don't chew up your food enough, the same thing could happen.

Our bodies know that something has "gone down the wrong pipe," and we automatically choke. That usually solves the problem.

WORDS to KNOW

trachea: Your windpipe, the tube where the air goes back and forth to your lungs.

esophagus: The tube that leads between your mouth and your stomach.

Furniture Dance

In this round, family members come up with pieces of furniture. Some examples are "desk," "bed," and "chair." As you go, you'll get to harder ones like hassock and valance!

Salad Time

Have each person come up with the name of a vegetable. For example, "turnip." And then "carrot." And then "tomato." And then "broccoli." And so on.

Ghost

Since you're holding the book, you get to start. But that means you need to read the directions, too!

This game is a little hard to explain but easy to play. Think of any word that's not a name—but don't tell anyone what it is. Then say the first letter out loud. The next family member adds a letter—and must be thinking of a real word that has that first and that second letter. The third person adds a letter, and makes sure the three letters do *not* spell a real word all on their own. They still have to be part of a longer real word. As the letters add up, it gets harder and harder to avoid spelling out a word when you add a letter!

The first person who is forced to spell out a word (or who does so accidentally) gets the letter "G." If a person is stuck and cannot think of a letter to add without spelling a word, that person may be tempted to "fake it" and say any letter that doesn't make a word. You can challenge that trickster—if he or she isn't thinking of a real word, then he or she gets a "G" also.

Once a word ends, the next person in line begins with a new word, and the game goes on. The first person to lose five times and spell out "GHOST" loses.

CUL8R

Some drivers like to choose a combination of letters and numbers for their license plate that sends a message. These are called "vanity plates." Perhaps their message will tell you about something they like or what they do for work. Can you correctly match the following people with their license plates? HINT: Having trouble? Try reading the plates out loud. Single letters can be used to represent a whole word. Sometimes numbers are used as part of a word. For example "CUL8R" is "See You Later."

IMAKID

Pediatrician
Big family
Person with bad memory
Comedian
Patient person
Impatient person
Lonely tennis player
Mom's reminder before a trip
Patriotic person
Family who likes to skate
Polite person
Computer person

US4EVR	XQZME	SK8RS
TOTDOC	I4GOT	HRDDRV
H82W8	IMFUNE	5KIDZ
1OSNE1	W8NC	PB4UGO

The Name Game

The leader names a famous person, such as George Bush. The next player uses the first initial of the last name (B) to start the first name of his person, Barney Rubble. The third player then comes up with an "R" name, Rosie O'Donnell. Just like "Famous People," you should agree on the rules first.

For some variations, try playing the "Geography" version. In "Geography," the last letter of the first word gives you the first letter of the next word. For example, Paris, then San Diego, then Ontario. To keep the game really moving, reverse directions if the first and last letters are the same (as in Ontario).

FUN FACT

Why Is Your Brother Burping?

Burping starts in the stomach, which can probably hold two to three cups of food. This includes the candy bar your brother just shoved down. It also includes that peanut butter sandwich he ate before—as long ago as four to five hours. (It looks more like a slimy blob than a sandwich by now, though.)

While your brother was eating, he swallowed some air, too. It just went down to the stomach with the food. But if he gulped air by eating fast, he swallowed too much. And if he drank a soda pop, he got way too much air—those bubbles have lots of carbon dioxide in them.

Maybe your brother filled up his stomach just a little too full, with a combination of food and air. If he did, some of the air will come out as an **eructation!**

WORDS to KNOW

eructation: A fancy word for burping! Just try this word out on your family!

Foul Feast

Each player contributes the name of two foods—so that all of you together have made up the yuckiest dinner imaginable. Think "broccoli with swamp minnow sauce," "Boiled buffalo head," "slug sundae with chocolate sauce," and so on.

Animal Advantages

Tell each person to combine three things from three different animals that add up to a superanimal—and why these would be useful. For example—the speed of a cheetah, the swoop of an eagle, and the deep diving of a killer whale. Then come up with a name for that superanimal—for example, the "Cheegle Whale." Did you know that there were many of these combination animals in Greek and other mythologies? For instance, the centaur supposedly had the brains and chest of a person and the four legs and back of a horse.

Fake Excuses

Why did the laziest kid at school not hand in the homework on time? Go around thinking of ridiculous excuses, such as "my computer ate it," "I jumped off the roof to get to school faster and it landed in a puddle," etc.

Animal? Absolutely Not.

Each family member comes up with the name of an animal that he or she would *least* like to be—and tells why. "Swamp rat" and "desert scorpion" come to mind.

QUICK QUIZ

Quick Quiz

Is a burp flammable (that means it could cause a fire)?

Yes, it is. Some of what comes up in a burp is hydrogen. That is definitely flammable. Of course, there's not really enough gas in your brother's burp to turn him into a dragon!

Be an Auto-Inventor

Do you ever get really restless traveling for hours? (I'll bet you do!) Why not imagine some ways to make a car or plane more comfortable. Here are a few ideas to get you started.

• Fold-down trays for cars so you can write, draw, or eat, the way you do on an airplane.
• Little, skinny lamps attached to the back of the seats. Then you can read, while the little kids sleep, even though it's dark outside. They would also collapse, to keep them out of the way when you're not using them.
• Goldfish bowl, with real fish (and a real lid!) to entertain you.

• _____
• _____
• _____

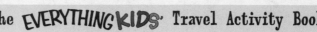
MPG

The letters "MPG" are an acronym (an abbreviation using the first letters) for "Miles Per Gallon." Figure out what this acronym stands for by looking at the picture.

HELP!

HELP!

SOS

Traveler: I always seem to get sick the night before I leave on a trip.

Travel Agent: Then why don't you leave a day earlier?

Rhyming Games

Car Rhymes

Come up with all the words you can that rhyme with "car." Remember that these words can be more than one syllable, like "Babar." Other words are star, mar, far, tar, etc.

How Does That Go?

Make up a new last line to a song, making sure it still rhymes with the line it's supposed to rhyme with. Here's an example:

Row, row, row your boat
Gently down the stream.
My brother isn't as big of a dope
As he must surely seem.

Limerick Time

Make up a limerick (a little goofy poem) with your sibling or parent—you each come up with every other line. It doesn't necessarily have to make sense. Here's an example:

There once was a boy named Bill.
He liked to eat burgers from the grill.
But sometimes he'd eat
Too close to the heat
And he'd drop his beef and then his dog would eat it up off of the ground—what a pill!

City Rhymes

Come up with a word or phrase that rhymes with the city you're in or are nearest to. For example, if you're near Chicago, you might say "Dr. Zhivago." An easier city might be "Minneapolis," which rhymes with "Indianapolis."

Sentence Rhyme

Make up a long sentence in which all the major words rhyme with every other. (Again, it doesn't necessarily have to make sense.) For example: "Ted and Fred said to shed your head or end up wedding the undead." Now start one with Joe and Moe . . .

Basic Poem

Make up a long, story-like poem that rhymes like this one:

Jon went walking to the store.
He tripped on a banana peel on the way.
He fell onto the floor.
He said it was a bad day.

Jon got up and kept going.
He made sure to watch for banana peels in front of him.
But soon it started snowing.
And the day began to look a bit grim.

Now start with "One fine day / It began to rain . . . "

FUN FACT

Has Your Foot "Gone to Sleep" on This Trip?

You know the feeling: the foot feels like a dead weight, floppy and weird. Then, when it "wakes up," it feels prickly for a few seconds. What's going on here?

The foot that went to "sleep" was probably the one you were sitting on for quite awhile. The weight of your body cut off part of the **circulation** in the foot—your blood couldn't flow in and out very well. The nerves in your foot got a little squashed also. And these nerves make the signals that help us feel our feet.

When you wiggled or stood up, the blood got flowing back into your foot again. The nerves sent out the message "yes—your foot is down here." As they "woke up," the prickly feeling came then quickly went away. Everything's back to normal.

WORDS to KNOW

circulation: The movement of your blood around your body. Circulation involves your heart, your lungs, your blood vessels, and more.

Weather Diary

Keep track of the temperature and other weather details from your trip. You can do this for every day of the vacation or for just a few days. The more the weather varies, the more interesting it will be (but 98° might make you too hot to feel all that interested).

Try to "take the day's temperature" at about the same time every day. Let's just pick noon.

Does your car have a thermometer? If it doesn't, listen to the radio (a local station) from five minutes before noon to five minutes after noon. They usually give weather information during those times. Or look for a bank or store sign that tells the time and temperature. You can use Fahrenheit or Celsius—or go all out and record both! Fill in a little chart like this:

Today is _____ (the date)
Temperature: ____°F or ____°C
It was (check one) ___sunny
          ___mostly sunny
          ___cloudy
          ___raining
          ___snowing
          ___sleeting
          ___stormy

Today is _____ (the date)
Temperature: ____°F or ____°C
It was (check one) ___sunny
          ___mostly sunny
          ___cloudy
          ___raining
          ___snowing
          ___sleeting
          ___stormy

Today is _____ (the date)
Temperature: ____°F or ____°C
It was (check one) ___sunny
          ___mostly sunny
          ___cloudy
          ___raining
          ___snowing
          ___sleeting
          ___stormy

Today is _____ (the date)
Temperature: ____°F or ____°C
It was (check one) ___sunny
          ___mostly sunny
          ___cloudy
          ___raining
          ___snowing
          ___sleeting
          ___stormy

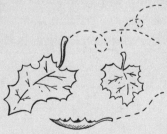

Chapter 3

Grab a Pen and Paper, and Settle In!

After rounds and rhymes, lots of teasing and laughing, and a few stops along the way, you've probably shouted "Enough!" Now it's time for some very quiet games—tell your parents and watch them smile. The drawing games, especially, are much harder for some people than others. But bring out the markers and don't be shy! Use these ideas to get you started.

Up Close and Personal

Draw what you see from where you're sitting. When you draw a room from within the room (and you can think of your car or plane as a very small room), you can draw the ceiling as sloping upward, toward the upper corners of the page. It's almost like you're looking down a narrow tunnel, or as though you're playing one of those "Doom"-type video games, where the tunnels scroll around and over you as you walk down them. Try it! It's hard, but fun.

The Postcard No One Has Ever Seen

Buy a blank postcard or cut one from a piece of cardboard and draw your own postcard. First, draw the things in the foreground, closest to you. Put them towards the bottom of the postcard. Since they're nearer to you, they're probably covering up the things that are farther away. Then draw in the things in the middle. Last, add the farthest away things, at the top of the postcard.

What should you put in? A big monster, or three suns, or a dozen moons shining over Disney World. Anything you want!

MPG

The letters "MPG" are an acronym (an abbreviation using the first letters) for "Miles Per Gallon." Figure out what this acronym stands for by looking at the picture.

Hey, this is my work!

MYOB

On the Road

Using the small pictures as clues, fill this puzzle with some familiar vehicles that you might see as you travel around. We have left you some V-R-O-O-Ms as a hint.

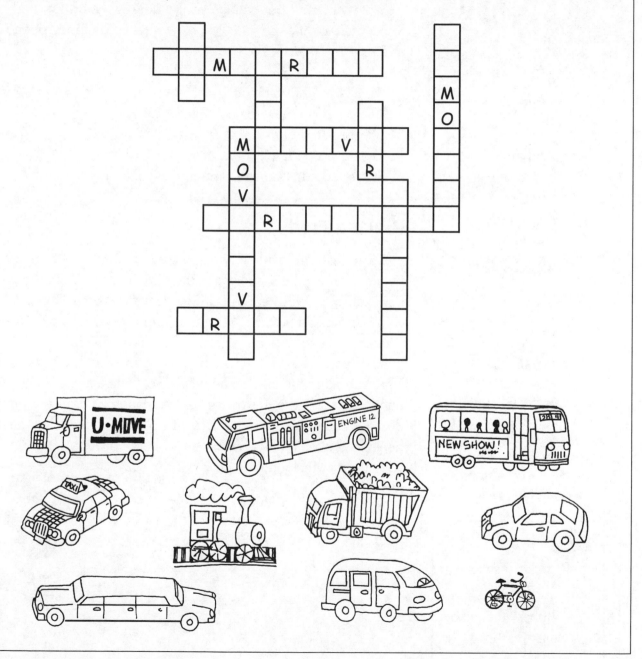

WORDS to KNOW

fictitious: Artificial or imagined, not true (like a fiction novel instead of a nonfiction history book).

Why did the silly traveler study in an airplane?

To get a higher education!

MPG

The letters "MPG" are an acronym (an abbreviation using the first letters) for "Miles Per Gallon." Figure out what this acronym stands for by looking at the picture.

"I can do this all by myself!"

PYO

We Had Fun, Out in the Sun

Write a poem about things you've done on your trip, and make pairs of lines rhyme. It doesn't have to be fancy-poetic or make perfect sense. For example:

We all flew into Billings.
We saw some cowboy hats.
We ate some pie,
And saw the big sky,
But we couldn't pay for dinner with shillings.

Pretend Fred

Make up—and write down—a story about an outrageous, **fictitious** character who lives in the city where you are today. For example, if you're in rural Kansas, write about "Tornado Tom." You might say that "Tornado Tom is a young boy who—without wanting to—makes tornadoes appear, wherever he goes. When Tom lived in Chicago, he found that the tornadoes were wrecking his city. So he moved to Kansas, where everything was spread out. Now, the tornadoes don't cause as much damage, because there's not as much stuff around for them to destroy." Doesn't this remind you of the myths you've read in school?

Let's Take a Long Walk

Draw a picture of yourself walking and carrying all of your luggage. Then figure out how long it would take you to walk the distance of your trip. If your trip has already been 500 miles and you could only walk 2½ miles per hour (with all that gear), it would take you about 200 hours. Do you think you could walk for fourteen hours a day? That would leave you nine hours per day to sleep, and one hour for either eating or resting. And even then, it would take you at least fourteen days to get as far as you are now.

Family Album

Aaron and Jason both wanted to take a picture of their parents at the scenic rest area. But somehow each picture turned out a little different! Can you find the nine differences between the two snapshots?

Word Search

In this word grid, see if you can find thirteen things you might see when driving along the coast. The words can go backward, forward, up, down, and diagonally.

BRIDGE
BUOY
FISHERMEN
KITES
LIFEGUARDS
LIGHTHOUSE
LOBSTER POT
ROWBOAT
SAILBOAT
SAND
SEAGULL
SURFERS
WAVES

```
S  S  S  A  I  L  B  O  A  T  S
L  D  E  E  G  D  I  R  B  E  L
O  R  R  T  S  H  E  S  V  I  L
B  O  E  A  I  L  L  A  G  S  L
S  W  S  E  U  K  W  H  A  S  U
T  B  H  E  L  G  T  L  S  B  G
E  O  Y  T  S  H  E  Y  H  E  A
R  A  S  A  O  E  A  F  O  S  E
P  T  N  U  H  O  R  E  I  U  S
O  D  S  U  R  F  E  R  S  L  B
T  E  F  I  S  H  E  R  M  E  N
```

Extra puzzle points: After you have circled all the listed words, read the leftover letters from left to right, and top to bottom. You will find a popular tongue twister!

Thanks for the Memories

Write a letter of appreciation to a grandparent or teacher. You don't have to have any special reason for writing it. For example, if it's summer, write a letter thanking your teacher for making the school year fun and interesting. Mention a few clever things the teacher had planned for your class to do during the last year.

If you haven't seen your grandparents in a while, tell them what you're doing, and where you are going on your trip. If you have just seen them, mention what you especially enjoyed doing with them when you visited.

A Caricature?

Draw someone who is traveling with you. You might try exaggerating a feature of that face. For example, if you think your sister has nice eyes, draw a face whose largest feature is the eyes. Or, you can make a different kind of caricature. If your brother is clumsy, draw a monkey with clown shoes on, slipping on a banana peel, and then title it something like "Jonathon, in his true form."

WORDS to KNOW

caricature: An exaggerated version of something, done in a funny way. Good caricatures usually pick one feature that really stands out, and then make it bigger. Be careful, though! You could do a good caricature of someone with big ears, or a big nose, but they might not like it. If you can, pick a really nice feature, and concentrate on that.

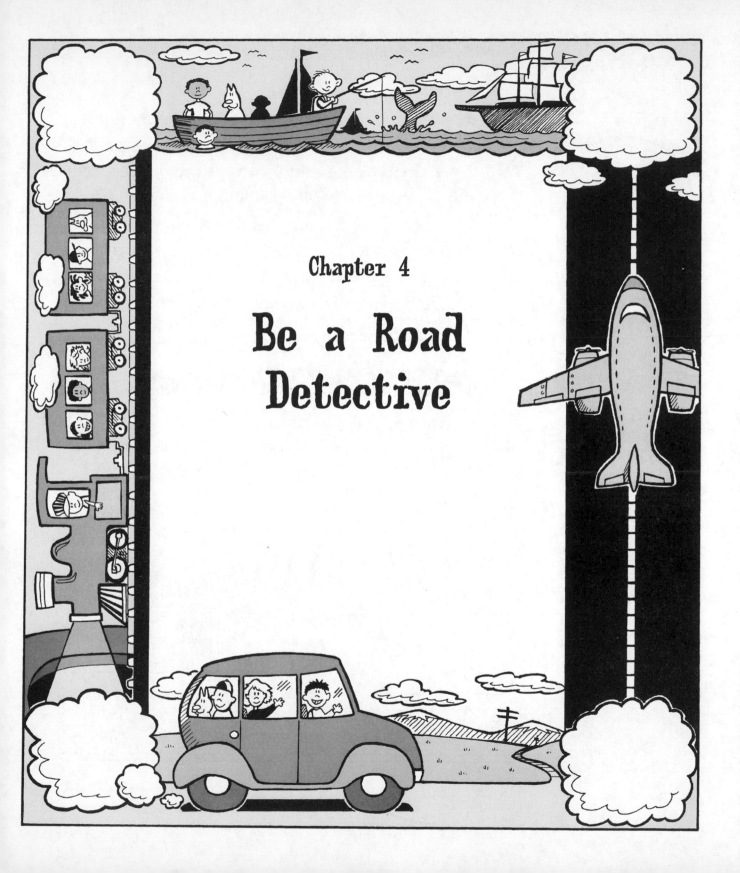

Chapter 4

Be a Road Detective

My daughter went on a cruise.

Jamaica?

No, she wanted to go!

What is different about where you are right now? Even though the gas stations and fast food places may look mostly the same, no whole country is *really* all the same. People eat reindeer in Alaska, and pecan rolls in the South. The yards have palm trees in Los Angeles, and evergreens in Maine. Well, you can be a detective and find quite a few of these differences. It's all in where you look.

Local Color

When you stop in the next town or city, buy a **local** newspaper. Some smaller towns have newspapers that only come out weekly, but most have "dailies." If you find a weekly, it probably won't be a thick paper.

WORDS to KNOW

local: Related to a specific and limited area; not general or widespread.

To find out more about where you are visiting, skip over the national stories (about the president and such) and the international stories (on Pakistan, England, or China). Look for articles about the area. Read the little stuff about the little league, or the high school principal who's retiring. The gardening or cooking column might be focused on local festivals, or food that's popular in that area. Even read about the crimes. Is there more or less crime than you hear about at home?

On road trips, ask the "rulers of the front seat" to flip around the radio dial until you find a local radio station. As you go along, the number and quality of available stations will change as you get nearer to different towns or cities. Listen to one station until you hear the local news report. What kinds of problems does the mayor have? What are people disagreeing about? What are they celebrating?

Now think: In what ways is this town or city different from where you live? You may want to talk this all over with the grownups. After a while, you might not see a new place as weird—just different.

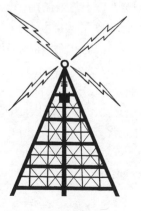

Word Search

In this word grid, see if you can find thirteen things you might spot when driving through the mountains. The words can go backwards, forwards, up, down, and diagonally.

DEER
EAGLE
FIREWOOD
HIKER
LOG CABIN
MOOSE
PINE CONE

PINE TREE
ROCKS
SKI AREA
SNOW
TRAIL
WATERFALL

```
E S P I N E T R E E F
I L N A E R A I K S I
E T G O I S T W W E R
N N T A W Y N A I N E
O E T H E O T U S A W
C N H I K E R D A N O
E D T W R E A E E N O
N T Y F S E I I E G D
I H A O T F L E E D T
P L O T A L S K C O R
L M L O G C A B I N L
```

Extra puzzle points: After you have circled all the listed words, read the leftover letters from left to right, and top to bottom. You will find a fast fact about Mount Everest, the world's tallest mountain!

MPG

The letters "MPG" are an acronym (an abbreviation using the first letters) for "Miles Per Gallon." Figure out what this acronym stands for by looking at the picture.

What is it?

I don't know, but it's moving fast!

UFO

Knock, knock.
Who's there?
Retakes.
Retakes who?
Retakes our time when we travel anywhere!

Games

Grocery Gumshoe

In case you didn't know, a "gumshoe" is a detective, *not* a person buying gum while wearing shoes or stepping on gum or something. The word dates back about a hundred years, to when people wore a type of soft-soled rubber shoe, called a gumshoe, that allowed them to walk around quietly.

Anyway, stop in a *real* grocery store in the next town. (Make sure it's not a gas station/convenience store. They usually sell mostly the same stuff all over the country.) Go into the grocery store and snoop around—especially the deli counter, fish counter, and bakery areas. What do they sell here that you don't typically see in your hometown? Some areas are known for their seafood or special fruits and vegetables. It's always interesting to see what's "normal" for other places, and sometimes it's nice to think about what's special about your home, too!

Web Detective

If your family has time, stop briefly in any Kinko's, Computer City, or Internet cafe—in any city. Use their computers to find the Web site of that city. (Some towns may be too small to have Web sites.) What does the site tell you about this city? Look for things like upcoming events, tourist sites that you *have to* see, and city news. Walking tours and parks are a great way to see a city and watch the people, too.

You can also search online while traveling in a car or train if you've brought a laptop along. Some hotels may have an Internet connection available. If there is a fee, ask your parents first if it's okay to go online.

Beep Beep

The Dot family has spent the day at a giant craft fair. Now it's time to go home, but where is their car? Look around carefully—Papa Dot had it painted a special way, and even got a special license plate. Can you spot the Dots' car, and find the family a path to it?

Restaurant Investigations

If you are someplace for a few days, try to go to a "real" restaurant at lunchtime. (Hint: McDonald's, Arby's, and the like are not real in this sense!) The restaurant should be one that looks like it's run by people from that town, serves what people in that town like, and attracts those townspeople.

Go in, check it out, order, and eat. Very **discreetly** look around, road detective! You may want to ask some of the people in the restaurant questions about themselves, or their town. Remember, though, that you are talking to strangers, so make sure a grownup you're traveling with is there and knows what you're doing. You're in a restaurant, of course, so try not to interrupt people who are eating. Politely introduce yourself, and ask some questions like these:

Do you live in this town?
What do you like best about it?
What do people do on the weekends for fun?
What makes your town different from other places?

Usually, people like talking about themselves and things they know about. If you start a polite conversation, and are interested in discovering some things, most people will be happy to talk to you, too.

discreetly: Quietly, without drawing attention. If you need to sneeze at the dinner table, it's polite to discreetly turn your head and cover your mouth, and not make a big scene sneezing on everyone else's plate.

Are You Daydreaming?

Scientists estimate that the average person spends five hours per day daydreaming! Of course, this time doesn't come in big chunks—most daydreams are only a second or two long. And you're usually doing something else at the same time. Since we have about 10 billion brain cells, we can do two things at once!

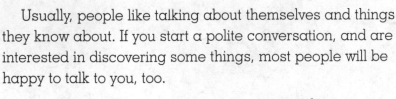

Chapter 5

Read-Alouds

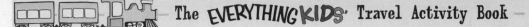
For a different activity, try the beginnings of four cool books. They are all old, all classics, and all terrific. Two of these great stories feature boys as heroes, and two feature girls. But everyone should enjoy all four adventures.

If you're in the car, take turns reading them out loud. Or, if you're on a plane or a train, read them to yourself. It can be fun to try them out—and, if you like them, you can read the rest later. These stories are a lot older than Harry Potter or American Girls, and exciting in a different way!

If enough people in the family love the book, just stop at a bookstore in the next town or city. Since these stories are classics, most bookstores will probably have paperback copies, which aren't very expensive. Then you can read a couple of chapters a day.

The Swiss Family Robinson
by Johann Wyss

✦ Chapter 1: Shipwrecked and Alone ✦

For many days we had been tempest-tossed. Six times had the darkness closed over a wild and terrific scene, and returning light as often brought but renewed distress, for the raging storm increased in fury until on the seventh day all hope was lost.

We were driven completely out of our course; no conjecture could be formed as to our whereabouts. The crew had lost heart, and were utterly exhausted by incessant labour.

The riven masts had gone by the board, leaks had been sprung in every direction, and the water, which rushed in, gained upon us rapidly.

Instead of reckless oaths, the seamen now uttered frantic cries to God for mercy, mingled with strange and often ludicrous vows, to be performed should deliverance be granted.

Every man on board alternately commended his soul to his Creator, and strove to bethink himself of some means of saving his life.

My heart sank as I looked round upon my family in the midst of these horrors. Our four young sons were overpowered by terror. "Dear children," said I, "if the Lord will, He can save us even from this fearful peril; if not, let us calmly yield our lives into His hand, and think of the joy and blessedness of finding ourselves for ever and ever united in that happy home above."

At these words my weeping wife looked bravely up, and, as the boys clustered round her, she began to cheer and encourage them with calm and loving words. I rejoiced to see her fortitude, though my heart was ready to break as I gazed on my dear ones.

We knelt down together, one after another praying with deep earnestness and emotion. Fritz, in particular, besought help and deliverance for his dear parents and brothers, as though quite forgetting himself.

Our hearts were soothed by the never-failing comfort of childlike confiding prayer, and the horrors of our situation seemed less overwhelming. "Ah," thought I, "the Lord will hear our prayer! He will help us."

Amid the roar of the thundering waves I suddenly heard the cry of "land! land!" while at the same instant the ship struck with a frightful shock, which threw everyone to the deck, and seemed to threaten her immediate destruction.

Dreadful sounds betokened the breaking up of the ship, and the roaring waters poured in on all sides.

Then the voice of the captain was heard above the tumult, shouting, "Lower away the boats! We are lost!"

"Lost!" I exclaimed, and the word went like a dagger to my heart; but seeing my children's terror renewed, I composed myself, calling out cheerfully, "Take courage, my boys! We are all above water yet. There is the land not far off, let us do our best to reach it. You know God helps those that help themselves!" With that, I left them and went on deck. What was my horror when through the foam and spray I beheld

the only remaining boat leave the ship, the last of the seamen spring into her and push off, regardless of my cries and entreaties that we might be allowed to share their slender chance of preserving their lives. My voice was drowned in the howling of the blast, and even had the crew wished it, the return of the boat was impossible.

Casting my eyes despairingly around, I became gradually aware that our position was by no means hopeless, inasmuch as the stern of the ship containing our cabin was jammed between two high rocks, and was partly raised from among the breakers which dashed the fore-part to pieces. As the clouds of mist and rain drove past, I could make out, through rents in the vaporous curtain, a line of rocky coast, and, rugged as it was, my heart bounded towards it as a sign of help in the hour of need. Yet the sense of our lonely and forsaken condition weighed heavily upon me as I returned to my family, constraining myself to say with a smile, "Courage, dear ones! Although our good ship will never sail more, she is so placed that our cabin will remain

above water, and tomorrow, if the wind and waves abate, I see no reason why we should not be able to get ashore."

These few words had an immediate effect on the spirits of my children, who at once regarded our problematical chance of escaping as a happy certainty, and began to enjoy the relief from the violent pitching and rolling of the vessel.

My wife, however, perceived my distress and anxiety in spite of my forced composure, and I made her comprehend our real situation, greatly fearing the effect of the intelligence on her nerves. Not for a moment did her courage and trust in Providence forsake her, and on seeing this, my fortitude revived.

"We must find some food, and take a good supper," said she, "it will never do to grow faint by fasting too long. We shall require our utmost strength tomorrow." Night drew on apace, the storm was as fierce as ever, and at intervals we were startled by crashes announcing further damage to our unfortunate ship. "God will help us soon now, won't He, father?" said my youngest child.

"You silly little thing," said Fritz, my eldest son, sharply, "don't you know that we must not settle what God is to do for us? We must have patience and wait His time."

"Very well said, had it been said kindly, Fritz, my boy. You too often speak harshly to your brothers, although you may not mean to do so."

A good meal being now ready, my youngsters ate heartily, and retiring to rest were speedily fast asleep. Fritz, who was

of an age to be aware of the real danger we were in, kept watch with us. After a long silence, "Father," said he, "don't you think we might contrive swimming-belts for mother and the boys? With those we might all escape to land, for you and I can swim."

"Your idea is so good," answered I, "that I shall arrange something at once, in case of an accident during the night."

We immediately searched about for what would answer the purpose, and fortunately got hold of a number of empty flasks and tin canisters, which we connected two and two together so as to form floats sufficiently buoyant to support a person in the water, and my wife and young sons each willingly put one on. I then provided myself with matches, knives, cord, and other portable articles, trusting that, should the vessel go to pieces before daylight, we might gain the shore, not wholly destitute.

Fritz, as well as his brothers, now slept soundly. Throughout the night my wife and I maintained our prayerful watch, dreading at every fresh sound some fatal change in the position of the wreck.

At length the faint dawn of day appeared, the long weary night was over, and with thankful hearts we perceived that the gale had begun to moderate; blue sky was seen above us, and the lovely hues of sunrise adorned the eastern horizon.

I aroused the boys, and we assembled on the remaining portion of the deck, when they, to their surprise, discovered that no one else was on board.

"Hello, papa! What has become of everybody? Are the sailors gone? Have they taken away the boats? Oh, papa! Why did they leave us behind? What can we do by ourselves!"

"My good children," I replied, "we must not despair, although we seem deserted. See how those on whose skill and good faith we depended have left us cruelly to our fate in the hour of danger. God will never do so. He has not forsaken us, and we will trust Him still. Only let us bestir ourselves, and each cheerily do his best. Who has anything to propose?"

"The sea will soon be calm enough for swimming," said Fritz.

"And that would be all very fine for you," exclaimed Ernest, "but think of mother and the rest of us! Why not build a raft and all get on shore together?"

"We should find it difficult, I think, to make a raft that would carry us safe to shore. However, we must contrive something, and first let each try to procure what will be of most use to us."

If you were about to be stranded on an island, what would you do? Mr. Robinson found matches, cord, and a knife to bring on shore. What other things left on a ship might be useful to the family?

Little Women
by Louisa May Alcott

✦ Chapter 1: Playing Pilgrims ✦

"Christmas won't be Christmas without any presents," grumbled Jo, lying on the rug.

"It's so dreadful to be poor!" sighed Meg, looking down at her old dress.

"I don't think it's fair for some girls to have plenty of pretty things, and other girls nothing at all," added little Amy, with an injured sniff.

"We've got father and mother and each other," said Beth, contentedly, from her corner.

The four young faces on which the firelight shone brightened at the cheerful words, but darkened again as Jo said sadly:

"We haven't got father, and shall not have him for a long time." She didn't say "perhaps never," but each silently added it, thinking of father far away, where the fighting was.

Nobody spoke for a minute; then Meg said in an altered tone: "You know the reason mother proposed not having any presents this Christmas was because it is going to be a hard winter for everyone; and she thinks we ought not to spend money for pleasure when our men are suffering so in the army. We can't do much, but we can make our little sacrifices, and ought to do it gladly. But I am afraid I don't," and Meg shook her head, and she thought regretfully of all the pretty things she wanted.

"But I don't think the little we should spend would do any good. We've each got a dollar, and the army wouldn't be much helped by our giving that. I agree not to expect anything from mother or you, but I do want to buy Undine and

Sintram for myself; I've wanted it so long," said Jo, who was a bookworm.

"I planned to spend mine on new music," said Beth, with a little sigh, which no one heard but the hearth-brush and kettle-holder.

"I shall get a nice box of Faber's drawing pencils; I really need them," said Amy, decidedly.

"Mother didn't say anything about our money, and she won't wish us to give up everything. Let's each buy what we want, and have a little fun; I'm sure we work hard enough to earn it," cried Jo, examining the heels of her shoes in a gen-tlemanly manner.

"I know *I* do—teaching those tiresome children nearly all day when I am longing to enjoy myself at home," began Meg, in the complaining tone again.

"You don't have half such a hard time as I do," said Jo. "How would you like to be shut up for hours with a nervous, fussy old lady, who keeps you trotting, is never satisfied, and worries you till you're ready to fly out of the window or cry?"

"It's naughty to fret; but I do think washing dishes and keeping things tidy is the worst work in the world. It makes me cross; and my hands get so stiff, I can't practice well at all"; and Beth looked at her rough hands with a sigh that anyone could hear that time.

"I don't believe any of you suffer as I do," cried Amy; "for you don't have to go to school with impertinent girls, who plague you if you don't know your lessons, and laugh at your

dresses, and label your father if he isn't rich, and insult you when your nose isn't nice."

"If you mean *libel*, I'd say so, and not talk about *labels*, as if papa was a pickle bottle," advised Jo, laughing.

"I know what I mean, and you needn't be *satirical* about it. It's proper to use good words, and improve your *vocabulary*," returned Amy, with dignity.

"Don't peck at one another, children. Don't you wish we had the money papa lost when we were little, Jo? Dear me! How happy and good we'd be, if we had no worries!" said Meg, who could remember better times.

"You said, the other day, you thought we were a deal happier than the King children, for they were fighting and fretting all the time, in spite of their money."

"So I did, Beth. Well, I think we are; for, though we do have to work, we make fun for ourselves, and are a pretty jolly set, as Jo would say."

"Jo does use such slang words!" observed Amy, with a reproving look at the long figure stretched on the rug. Jo immediately sat up, put her hands in her pockets, and began to whistle.

"Don't, Jo; it's so boyish!"

"That's why I do it."

"I detest rude, unlady-like girls!"

"I hate affected, niminy-piminy chits!"

"Birds in their little nests agree," sang Beth, the peace maker, with such a funny face that both sharp voices softened to a laugh, and the "pecking" ended for that time.

"Really, girls, you are both to be blamed," said Meg, beginning to lecture in her elder-sisterly fashion. "You are old enough to leave off boyish tricks, and to behave better Josephine. It didn't matter so much when you were a little girl; but now you are so tall, and turn up your hair, you should remember that you are a young lady."

"I'm not! And if turning up my hair makes me one, I'll wear it in two tails till I'm twenty," cried Jo, pulling off the net, and shaking down her chestnut mane. "I hate to think I've got to grow up, and be Miss March and wear long gowns, and look as prim as a China aster! It's bad enough to be a girl, anyway, when I like boys' games and work and manners! I can't get over my disappointment in not being a boy; and it's worse than ever now, for I'm dying to go and fight with papa,

and I can only stay at home and knit, like a poky old woman!" And Jo shook the blue army sock till the needles rattled like castanets, and her ball bounded across the room.

"Poor Jo! It's too bad, but it can't be helped; so you must try to be contented with making your name boyish, and playing brother to us girls," said Beth, stroking the rough head at her knee with a hand that all the dish-washing and dusting in the world could not make ungentle in its touch.

If you could only have one gift over the holidays, what would it be? If you only had money to buy one thing, would you buy just one present, or would you wait until you had enough money to get presents for everyone?

"As for you, Amy," continued Meg, "you are altogether too particular and prim. Your airs are funny now; but you'll grow up an affected little goose, if you don't take care. I like your nice manners and refined ways of speaking when you don't try to be elegant; but your absurd words are as bad as Jo's slang."

"If Jo is a tomboy and Amy a goose, what am I, please?" asked Beth, ready to share the lecture.

"You're a dear, and nothing else," answered Meg, warmly; and no one contradicted her, for the "Mouse" was the pet of the family.

As young readers like to know "how people look," we will take this moment to give them a little sketch of the four sisters, who sat knitting away in the twilight, while the

December snow fell quietly without, and the fire crackled cheerfully within. It was a comfortable old room, though the carpet was faded and the furniture very plain; for a good picture hung on the wall, books filled the recesses, chrysanthemums and Christmas roses bloomed in the windows, and a pleasant atmosphere of home-peace pervaded it.

Margaret, the eldest of the four, was sixteen, and very pretty, being plump and fair, with large eyes, plenty of soft, brown hair, a sweet mouth, and white hands, of which she was rather vain. Fifteen-year-old Jo was tall, thin, and brown, and reminded one of a colt; for she never seemed to know what to do with her long limbs, which were very much in her way. She had a decided mouth, a comical nose, and sharp, gray eyes, which appeared to see everything, and were by turns fierce, funny, or thoughtful. Her long, thick hair was one

of beauty, but it was usually bundled into a net, to be out of her way. Round shoulders had Jo, big hands and feet, a fly-away look to her clothes, and the uncomfortable appearance of a girl who was rapidly shooting up into a woman, and didn't like it. Elizabeth—or Beth, as everybody called her—was a rosy, smooth-haired girl of thirteen, with a shy manner, a timid voice, and a peaceful expression, which was seldom disturbed. Her father called her "Little Tranquility," and the name suited her excellently; for she seemed to live in a happy world of her own, only venturing out to meet the few she trusted and loved. Amy, the youngest, was a most important person—in her own opinion at least. A regular snow-maiden, with blue eyes, and yellow hair, always carrying herself like a young lady mindful of her manners. What characters the four sisters were we will leave to be found out.

How would you describe your brothers or sisters? If you did a carica-ture, you already thought about what you notice most. But what about their hobbies and habits? Are they the same as yours, or different?

Treasure Island
by Robert Louis Stevenson

✦ Chapter 1: Old Sea Dog At the "Admiral Benbow" ✦

Squire Trelawney, Dr. Livesey, and the rest of these gentlemen having asked me to write down the whole particulars about Treasure Island, from the beginning to the end, keeping nothing back but the bearings of the island, and that only because there is still treasure not yet lifted, I take up my pen in the year of grace 17–, and go back to the time when my father kept the "Admiral Benbow" inn, and the brown old seaman, with the sabre cut, first took up his lodging under our roof.

I remember him as if it were yesterday, as he came plodding to the inn door, his sea chest following behind him in a handbarrow; a tall, strong, heavy, nut-brown man; his tarry

pigtail falling over the shoulders of his soiled blue coat; his hands ragged and scarred, with black, broken nails; and the sabre cut across one cheek, a dirty, livid white. I remember him looking round the cove and whistling to himself as he did so, and then breaking out in that old sea-song that he sang so often afterwards:

"Fifteen men on the dead man's chest—Yo-ho-ho, and a bottle of rum!" in the high, old tottering voice that seemed to have been tuned and broken at the capstan bars. Then he rapped on the door with a bit of stick like a handspike that he carried, and when my father appeared, called roughly for

a glass of rum. This, when it was brought to him, he drank slowly, like a connoisseur, lingering on the taste, and still looking about him at the cliffs and up at our signboard.

"This is a handy cove," says he, at length; "and a pleasant sittyated grog-shop. Much company, mate?" My father told him no, very little company, the more was the pity.

"Well, then," said he, "this is the berth for me. Here you matey," he cried to the man who trundled the barrow; "bring up alongside and help up my chest. I'll stay here a bit," he continued. "I'm a plain man; rum and bacon and eggs is what I want, and that head up there for to watch ships off. What you mought call me? You mought call me captain. Oh, I see what you're at—there"; and he threw down three or four gold pieces on the threshold. "You can tell me when I've worked through that," says he, looking as fierce as a commander.

And, indeed, bad as his clothes were, and coarsely as he spoke, he had none of the appearance of a man who sailed before the mast; but seemed like a mate or skipper accustomed to be obeyed or to strike. The man who came with the barrow told us the mail had set him down this morning before at the "Royal George"; that he had inquired what inns there were along the coast, and hearing ours well spoken of, I suppose, and described as lonely, had chosen it from the others for his place of residence. And that was all we could learn of our guest.

There may be times when your family has new guests visiting. What do you do to make them feel welcome? What interesting things in your home or neighborhood would you show them?

He was a very silent man by custom. All day he hung round the cove, or upon the cliffs, with a brass telescope; all evening he sat in a corner of the parlour next to the fire, and drank rum and water very strong. Mostly he would not speak when spoken to; only look up sudden and fierce, and blow through his nose like a foghorn; and we and the people who came about our house soon learned to let him be. Every day, when he came back from his stroll, he would ask if any sea-faring men had gone by along the road. At first we thought it was the want of company of his own kind that made him ask this question; but at last we began to see he was desirous to avoid them. When a seaman put up at the "Admiral Benbow" (as now and then some did, making by the coast road for

Bristol) he would look in at him through the curtained door before he entered the parlour; and he was always sure to be as silent as a mouse when any such was present. For me, at least, there was no secret about the matter; for I was, in a way, a sharer in his alarms. He had taken me aside one day, and promised me a silver fourpenny on the first of every month if I would only keep my "weather eye open for a seafaring man with one leg," and let him know the moment he appeared. Often enough, when the first of the month came round, and I applied to him for my wage, he would only blow through his nose at me, and stare me down; but before the week was out he was sure to think better of it, bring me my fourpenny piece, and repeat his orders to look out for "the seafaring man with one leg."

How that personage haunted my dreams, I need scarcely tell you. On stormy nights, when the wind shook the four corners of the house, and the surf roared along the cove and up the cliffs, I would see him in a thousand forms, and with a thousand diabolical expressions. Now the leg would be cut off at the knee, now at the hip, now he was a monstrous kind of a creature who had never had but one leg, and that in the middle of his body. To see him leap and run and pursue me over the hedge was the worst of nightmares. And altogether I paid pretty dear my monthly fourpenny piece, in the shape of these abominable fancies.

Sometimes you hear about things—people or creatures or places—that you have never seen. What do you imagine they are really like? Do you think they are better or worse than what you picture in your mind?

Alice in Wonderland
by Lewis Carroll

✦ Chapter 1: Down the Rabbit Hole ✦

Alice was beginning to get very tired of sitting by her sister on the bank, and of having nothing to do; once or twice she had peeped into the book her sister was reading, but it had no pictures or conversations in it, "and what is the use of a book," thought Alice "without pictures or conversation?"

So she was considering in her own mind (as well as she could, for the hot day made her feel very sleepy and stupid) whether the pleasure of making a daisy chain would be worth the trouble of getting up and picking the daisies, when suddenly a white rabbit with pink eyes ran close by her.

There was nothing so *very* remarkable in that; nor did Alice think it so very much out of the way to hear the Rabbit say to itself, "Oh dear! Oh dear! I shall be late!" (when she thought it over afterward it occurred to her that she ought to have wondered at this, but at the time it all seemed quite natural); but when the Rabbit actually *took a watch out of its waistcoat pocket*, and looked at it, and then hurried on, Alice started to her feet, for it flashed across her mind that she had never before seen a rabbit with either a waistcoat-pocket, or a watch to take out of it, and, burning with curiosity, she ran across the field after it, and fortunately was just in time to see it pop down a large rabbit hole under the hedge.

In another moment down went Alice after it, never once considering how in the world she was to get out again. The rabbit hole went straight on like a tunnel for some way, and then dipped suddenly down, so suddenly that Alice had not a moment to think about stopping herself before she found herself falling down a very deep well.

What kind of rabbit would have a rabbit hole big enough for a girl to fit through? If you were falling down the well, what do you think it would feel like? Would it be slow, like going up a roller coaster, or fast and windy, like coming down the other side?

Either the well was very deep, or she fell very slowly, for she had plenty of time as she went down to look about her, and to wonder what was going to happen next. First, she tried to look down and make out what she was coming to, but it was too dark to see anything; then she looked at the sides of the well, and noticed that they were filled with cupboards and bookshelves; here and there she saw maps and pictures hung upon pegs. She took down a jar from one of the shelves as she passed; it was labeled "ORANGE MARMALADE," but to her great disappointment it was empty; she did not like to drop the jar for fear of killing somebody, so managed to put it into one of the cupboards as she fell past it.

"Well!" thought Alice to herself, "after such a fall as this, I shall think nothing of tumbling downstairs! How brave they'll all think me at home! Why, I wouldn't say anything about it even if I fell off the top of the house!" (Which was very likely true.)

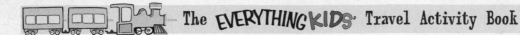
Down, down, down. Would the fall *never* come to an end? "I wonder how many miles I've fallen by this time?" she said aloud. "I must be getting somewhere near the centre of the earth. Let me see: that would be four thousand miles down, I think" (for, you see, Alice had learnt several things of this sort in her lessons in the schoolroom, and though this was not a very good opportunity for showing off her knowledge, as there was no one to listen to her, still it was good practice to say it over) "—yes, that's about the right distance—but then I wonder what Latitude or Longitude I've got to?" (Alice had no idea what Latitude was, or Longitude either, but thought they were nice grand words to say.)

Presently she began again. "I wonder if I shall fall right *through* the earth! How funny it'll seem to come out among the people that walk with their heads downward! The Antipathies, I think" (she was rather glad there *was* no one listening, this time, as it didn't sound at all the right word); "but I shall have to ask them what the name of the country is, you know. Please, Ma'am, is this New Zealand or Australia?" (and she tried to curtsey as she spoke—fancy *curtseying* as you're falling through the air! Do you think you could manage it?) "And what an ignorant little girl she'll think me for asking! No, it'll never do to ask; perhaps I shall see it written up somewhere."

Down, down, down. There was nothing else to do, so Alice soon began talking again. "Dinah'll miss me very much tonight, I should think!" (Dinah was the cat.) "I hope they'll remember her saucer of milk at teatime. Dinah my dear! I wish you were down here with me! There are no mice in the air, I'm afraid, but you might catch a bat, and that's very like a mouse, you know. But do cats eat bats, I wonder?" And here Alice began to get rather sleepy, and went on saying to herself, in a dreamy sort of way, "Do cats eat bats? Do cats eat bats?" and sometimes, "Do bats eat cats?" for, you see, as she couldn't answer either question, it didn't much matter which way she put it. She felt that she was dozing off, and had just begun to dream that she was walking hand in hand with Dinah, and saying to her very earnestly, "Now, Dinah,

tell me the truth: did you ever eat a bat?" when suddenly, thump! thump! down she came upon a heap of sticks and dry leaves, and the fall was over.

Alice was not a bit hurt, and she jumped up on to her feet in a moment: she looked up, but it was all dark overhead; before her was another long passage, and the White Rabbit was still in sight, hurrying down it. There was not a moment to be lost: away went Alice like the wind, and was just in time to hear it say, as it turned a comer, "Oh my ears and whiskers, how late it's getting!" She was close behind it when she turned the corner, but the Rabbit was no longer to be seen: she found herself in a long, low hall, which was lit up by a row of lamps hanging from the roof.

There were doors all round the hall, but they were all locked. And when Alice had been all the way down one side and up the other, trying every door, she walked sadly down the middle, wondering how she was ever to get out again.

There are a lot of places where you could get separated from the people you are with—especially when you are traveling in strange places. You could be in a crowd, or you could be in a long hallway, like Alice. What would you do if you got separated from your family and didn't know where to go? It's a good idea to talk to your parents about getting lost, so you'll know what to do so they can find you.

Chapter 6

Sing-Alongs

Keep It Festive

If you're traveling over a holiday, theme songs will get everyone excited. You've probably learned songs in school that your brothers, sisters, or friends know, too. And you can teach them to your parents if they haven't heard them before.

Religious holiday songs are very common, of course, but try to think of songs for Halloween, Thanksgiving, and the Fourth of July.

MPG

The letters "MPG" are an acronym (an abbreviation using the first letters) for "Miles Per Gallon." Figure out what this acronym stands for by looking at the picture.

LOL

Are you driving after dark, or early in the morning? Or are you just a little bit restless or hungry? A family sing-along can be just the thing to perk everyone up. Start with these, and you'll be able to think of many more once you get going.

Yankee Doodle

Oh, Yankee Doodle went to town,
A-riding on a pony
He stuck a feather in his hat
And called it macaroni.

Yankee Doodle, doodle doo,
Yankee Doodle Dandy,
All the lads and lassies are
As sweet as sugar candy.

The Star Spangled Banner

Oh, say, can you see, by the dawn's early light,
What so proudly we hail'd at the twilight's last gleaming!
Whose broad stripes and bright stars, thro' the perilous night,
O'er the ramparts we watch'd were so gallantly streaming!

And the rockets red glare, the bombs bursting in air,
Gave proof thro' the night that our flag was still there.

Oh, say, does that Star Spangled Banner yet wave
O'er the land of the free and the home of the brave!

Pit Stop

No matter if you travel to city, country, seacoast, or mountain, there is one thing you need to get everywhere you go. Connect the dots to find out what.

Home on the Range

Oh, give me a home where the buffalo roam,
Where the deer and the antelope play;
Where seldom is heard a discouraging word,
And the skies are not cloudy all day.

Home, home on the range, where the deer and the antelope play;
Where seldom is heard a discouraging word,
And the skies are not cloudy all day.

Did you hear the joke about the express train?

Never mind—you just missed it!

Pop! Goes the Weasel

All around the cobbler's bench, the monkey chased the weasel;
The monkey thought 'twas all in fun, Pop! goes the weasel.
I've no time to wait or sign, no patience to wait 'til bye and bye;
Kiss me quick, I'm off; good-bye, Pop! goes the weasel.

I've Been Working on the Railroad

I've been working on the railroad,
All the livelong day,
I've been working on the railroad,
Just to pass the time away.
Don't you hear the whistle blowing,
Rise up so early in the morn;
Don't you hear the captain shouting,

"Dinah, blow your horn!"
Dinah, won't you blow, Dinah won't you blow, Dinah won't you
blow your horn.
Dinah, won't you blow, Dinah won't you blow, Dinah won't you
blow your horn.
Someone's in the kitchen with Dinah,
Someone's in the kitchen I know,
Someone's in the kitchen with Dinah,
strummin' on the old banjo, and singin'
Fee-fi-fidd-lee-i-o, fee-fi-fidd-lee-i-o
fee-fi-fidd-lee-i-o, strummin' on the old banjo.

And don't forget "When the Saints Go Marching In," "The
Yellow Rose of Texas," and "Oh, Beautiful, For Spacious Skies."

Make Up a Song

Why not make up your own song about where you are? Think first, and make a little list of some of the things you're seeing. Also list some of the funny names of the towns. And don't forget to add a few of the silly things your brother has said on this part of your trip.

Once you have a list, decide if you want to make up the music—or use the tune of a song you already know. "Sunny day, pushing the clouds away, I'm on my way," etc. But put in your own words.

Sing it for your family—and not too loud!

Batty Billboard

Driving along you will sometimes see an old billboard that has lost a few letters. The message left behind can be hard to read! See if you can fit the fallen letters and word-parts back into this billboard so you can read the message. BE CAREFUL—some letters have fallen sideways or upside-down.

```
_RAD__  __OB'S BIG
  HO_  __ LE
 _HIS  ___RED__LY
SUP__  SA__  W___
ON__  LAS_  A VE__
   __ORT  TIM_.
 _HOP  _OR  _HOE_
    —  _OW!
```

FUN FACT

Most-Used Interstates in America

Interstate 5: Bellingham, WA, to San Diego, CA

Interstate 15: Sweetgrass, MT, to San Diego, CA

Interstate 45: Dallas, TX, to Galveston, TX

Interstate 55: Chicago, IL, to Kenner, LA

Interstate 75: Mackinaw City, MI, to Naples, FL

Interstate 95: Houlton, ME, to Miami, FL

Interstate 94: Port Huron, MI, to Billings, MT

Interstate 90: Boston, MA, to Seattle, WA

Interstate 80: New York, NY, to San Francisco, CA

Interstate 70: Baltimore, MD, to Cove Fort, UT

Interstate 10: Jacksonville, FL, to Los Angeles, CA

Did you know . . . The interstate highways (not the state or county ones) that run east-west were all given even numbers. The interstates that run north-south are all odd numbers. What do you notice about the order of the numbers?

Take the Lead

Teach your family *all* of your camp, religious, or club songs. It could be "Kitch-i-yappi, Kitch-i-yappi, YMCA Day Camp," or "By the Shores of Lake Alligator, in the Sunset, by the Campfire." Many camp and folk songs are so old that your parents may know different verses. Get them to teach you the way they sang it, and you can do rounds!

MPG

The letters "MPG" are an acronym (an abbreviation using the first letters) for "Miles Per Gallon." Figure out what this acronym stands for by looking at the picture.

HURRY! Mail this right away!

Don't wait!

ASAP

Ninety-nine Bottles of . . .

Okay, everybody knows the tune, and everybody knows that there is a whole lot of beer involved. And you probably also know that as you get down to about seventy-five bottles (that's twenty-five verses, already!), the average parent wants to scream.

But you're creative! You're going to change the game to keep it interesting for everyone. Every time you go down one number (such as ninety-nine, ninety-eight, ninety-seven, and so on), think of a different beverage or liquid! For example, start with ninety-nine bottles of beer, then ninety-eight bottles of Coke, on down to twenty bottles of Johnson's Baby Shampoo on the wall. Take turns thinking of the new item, until everyone runs out of ideas. Then, and this rule is very clear, you HAVE TO STOP SINGING THAT SONG!

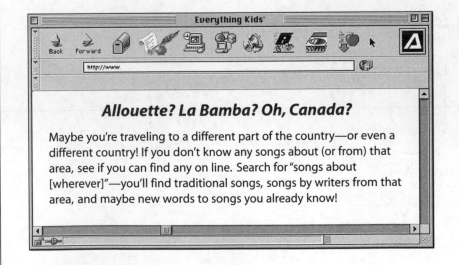

Allouette? La Bamba? Oh, Canada?

Maybe you're traveling to a different part of the country—or even a different country! If you don't know any songs about (or from) that area, see if you can find any on line. Search for "songs about [wherever]"—you'll find traditional songs, songs by writers from that area, and maybe new words to songs you already know!

Chapter 7

Go Creative

WORDS to KNOW

utopia: An imaginary place, often with ideal and perfect laws and government.

FUN FACT

Ice Cream Invention

The Ben & Jerry's ice cream called Chubby Hubby was "invented" as a practical joke. Two friends made up a flavor, found the ingredients, and served their creation. When people tasted the new ice cream, they liked it! The friends sent the idea to Ben & Jerry's, and now it's an official flavor.

Most of the games you've been playing get you to think fast, have fun, and keep busy. Now, add in some serious imagination and creativity. You can name a new kind of ice cream, and talk about what's in it and why those things would taste good together. Make up a slogan—even a way to advertise, or get people interested in your creation.

Or, you can create a whole new country—maybe a **utopia**. Would you have a new language, or use a combination of languages that already exist? If you created a country, where would it be? Would you want to be the ruler?

The best thing about these games is that you can play out loud, and talk about them with people in the car. Or you can just think about them if you are on a plane, or train, or everybody's sleeping.

Who Parked Where?

Three cars are parked next to each other in a rest area. By reading the clues below, can you tell which people are going to get into which vehicle, the color of the vehicle, and what state they are from? HINT: Use the grid provided to help figure out the answers.

- The man with a dog is not in a silver truck and is not from New York.
- The blue vehicle is not from Maine.
- The family in the red vehicle is not from Maine or Ohio.

- The twin sisters are in a truck with a Maine license plate.
- The sports car is from New York.
- The van is not silver or red.

	vehicle	state	color
man with dog			
twin sisters			
family			

Games

What If We Looked Different?

What would we do if . . .

. . . we had no thumbs?

. . . we had no hair?

. . . we had inline skates or scooters instead of feet?

. . . we had webbed hands like ducks?

. . . we had only one arm?

. . . we had only one leg?

. . . we had no noses?

. . . people were all nocturnal, like owls?

. . . we had four eyes (two on the back of our heads)?

What other strange possibilities can you think of?

What If the World Were Weirder?

What would we do if . . .

. . . trees could eat regular food?

. . . people could fly but not walk?

. . . dogs could talk?

. . . nobody ever died?

. . . something else grew on trees, rather than leaves?

. . . candy grew on the ground, instead of grass?

. . . everything were a different color?

. . . it rained something else instead of water?

. . . people were born old and got younger every year?

. . . gravity pulled everything up instead of down?

. . . nobody ever got mad or sad?

FUN FACT

Faster Than a Speeding Bullet!

- Light travels at 186,000 miles per second.
- Race drivers at the Indianapolis 500 reach 225 mph on the straightaways.
- The record speed for a car driving on land is at Black Rock Desert in Nevada, where a jet-powered car broke the sound barrier on land, traveling one mile at 763 mph.
- Cheetahs, big cats of Africa, can sprint at up to 68.4 mph.

Word Search

In this word grid, see if you can find fifteen things you might spot when driving down a country road. The words can go backwards, forwards, up, down, and diagonally.

BARN
CHICKENS
CORN FIELD
CROW
FARMHOUSE
GARDEN
GAZEBO
HAY WAGON
OLD DOG
PICKET FENCE
POND
SILO
TIRE SWING
TRACTOR
WOODPILE

```
E T I R E S W I N G B
T C T R A C T O R A O
E W N G E T W O R C S
S O G E T O O N O G N
U O A T F L H R E O E
O D Z O I T N T P D K
H P E S H F E O E D C
M I B R I S N K I L I
R L O E D D E ☺ C O H
A E L G A R D E N I C
F D N O G A W Y A H P
```

Extra puzzle points: After you have circled all the listed words, read the leftover letters from left to right, and top to bottom. You will find the answer to this riddle: Why did the chicken cross the country road?

Name a New Kind of . . .

. . . strawberry ice cream
. . . lemon ice cream
. . . blueberry ice cream
. . . chocolate ice cream
. . . lemon pie
. . . butterscotch cake
. . . granola cereal

. . . soap
. . . toothpaste
. . . deodorant
. . . shampoo
. . . finger paint
. . . TV set

After you've named these new products, come up with a few of your own. See if other people can guess what the new product is based on the name you've created.

On an Airplane and Feeling Good

If you are on an airplane, you have the opportunity to be quite an artist. How? By decorating the spit-up bags that come in your seat pocket. If the bag is folded like a brown grocery bag, try creating a puppet or two (borrow more bags from family members if you need to). If you don't have magic markers or crayons, ask the flight attendant for some—or just use a pen or pencil.

You have to be "feeling good" for this activity—otherwise, you might need to grab that bag and use it the way the airline planned!

A Story about Five Things

If you're in the car, or in your hotel room on a rainy day, try this with your whole group. One person chooses any five things to "put in the middle" (a small toy truck, Mom's purse, a small drum, some keys, and a hairbrush, for example). Then, you each tell any story that includes those five items.

If you're older, you can do it with some objects that aren't physically there (the North Pole, a lion, a spoon, a shooting star, and the sun, for example). For more object ideas, look at the big list that follows . . . that will keep everyone busy!

A Book	A Card Table	A Blanket	
A Shoe	Your Coat	The TV Set	
Mom's Car	A Piece of Bread	A Hole in the Ground	Cottage Cheese
A Chair	A Stick	Applesauce	Your Bed
A Windowpane	A Scarf	A Big Box	A Huge Leaf

What else?

Parking Lot

The following code is called a "parking lot code" because each letter is parked in a space that has a unique shape. To send a message, draw the outline of the parking space each letter is in, including the dot if there is one. For example, here is how to send the message "LOOK AT THAT":

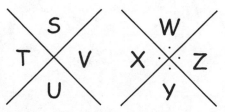

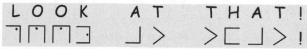

Can you decipher this secret message? HINT: You may hear this a lot on a long trip!

How Do *You* Remember It?

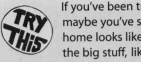

If you've been traveling for a long time, maybe you've sort of forgotten what your home looks like. Of course you remember the big stuff, like the color, and where the garage is, but what about hanging plants, shutters, or a weathervane? Do you have a basketball hoop? A fence or garden? A doghouse or shed?

Depending on where you're going on your trip, you may want to show people where you're from or what your favorite room looks like. Is it your bedroom? Think about the little details, like posters you have on the walls, things you keep on your desk or dresser, or whether you made your bed before you left. When you get home, compare your drawing to the real thing—it will be interesting to see what you've remembered.

If you can do even part of this stuff right, you probably have a very good eye for detail. You'd make a great police detective or mystery book writer!

What Else Could You Use It For?

A fireplace could be a raccoon home, a place to grow plants, a wastebasket, a hideout, a sleeping place, a rainwater catcher, a stove, a tree holder, a giant's stand-up resting place, a TV corner, and so on.

This list might be a good starting place for you. Do any of those things have other uses?

Weirdo Country

If we could create a whole new country, what would it be like there? (One might rain sunflower seeds, have parents who are smaller than children, have dogs that eat trash and sprout purple trees.) What would yours be like? What would you name it?

It's Like a Simile

Take turns thinking of similies—how one thing is like another—which is another way to build a poem. Remind everyone to be wild, and begin with comparisons like the following:

The clouds today are like . . . a scoop of vanilla ice cream, or a puddle of spilled milk?

FUN FACT

What Is Thunder?

Thunder is the sound made by the lightning. But why is a lightning bolt loud? Believe it or not, a lightning bolt is hotter than the surface of the sun—it can reach 27,000 degrees Fahrenheit. This heat makes the air around the lightning bolt expand out fast. This expansion produces shock waves that we hear as sound. If you're especially near to a lightning bolt, you're also more likely to get a direct shock wave—a big thunderclap.

What would you get if you crossed a bridge with a car?

You'd get to the other side!

Appendix

Cool Stuff,
State-by-State

here the heck are you going? If you're traveling in the United States, you'll find information about the state, cool history of the state, and some cool science fun facts about the state.

This section divides the United States into four regions, with a map at the beginning of each group. You can see where a specific state is, and you can also read about states that are near the one you're in.

You should read about your home state too!

West

Alaska

- Alaska was "discovered" by the Russians in 1741. They sold this almost unexplored place to the United States in 1867. Gold was discovered in 1898, and in 1968, most of the state's oil reserves were discovered.
- *peninsula:* An area of land that is surrounded by water on three sides.

The United States' largest and most northern state, Alaska, is a **peninsula**. The Arctic Ocean is to the north, and the Pacific Ocean is on the west and the south coasts. On the east, Alaska borders British Columbia, Canada.

Alaska has more state parks—and more acres of national parks and national forests—than any other state. In addition to volcanoes and glaciers, Alaska has the highest mountain in the United States, Mt. Denali (also called Mt. McKinley).

Anchorage, which has about 250,000 people, is by far the largest city in Alaska. The capital, Juneau, is the third largest city and has only about 30,000 people living in it.

Arizona

- The frontier here was warlike in the mid-1800s. Geronimo was fighting frontiersmen. And the gunfight at the O.K. Corral took place in Tombstone, Arizona.
- Kitt Peak Observatory is one of the United States' top astronomy observatories. Up high on a mountain and in the dry Arizona air, it is easier to see through the "blanket" of the Earth's atmosphere, way out to the stars.

This desert state is known for its sun, dry air, canyons, mountains, and Native American land. It has the most square miles of land owned by Native Americans of any state in the country.

Despite its southern latitude and huge deserts, Arizona has the snowiest metropolitan area in the United States. Flagstaff, Arizona, gets just over 100 inches of snow in a year, on average. Why? It is perched on a small mountain, almost like a castle, "collecting" snow.

Arizona may be best known as the home of the Grand Canyon, the biggest canyon in the United States. Phoenix is the state capital and is also the largest city, with a population of about 1.2 million people.

California

The northern California coast has huge redwood trees, also called sequoias. Some are 300 feet high! The Lava Beds National Monument is also in northern California, south of the town Tulelake. All the volcanoes here seem dead (or **dormant**), but they've left fields of dark lava, and about 200 lava caves.

North of San Francisco, the Point Reyes National Seashore is an astounding mix of cliffs, surf, and forest. In this general area, you can walk along the San Andreas Fault. The planet can split along this **fault**, which would probably cause a major earthquake!

California has the largest population of all fifty states, with about 33 million people. Sacramento is the capital, but Los Angeles is the state's biggest city, with about 3.8 million people within the city limits, and 9.9 million in the county!

- **dormant:** Temporarily or seemingly inactive. Dormant volcanoes erupt rarely; extinct ones don't erupt at all.
- **fault:** A crack between two slabs of rock in the earth's crust. These cracks and fractures are weak spots where earthquakes are most likely to occur.

Colorado

Colorado has the highest average elevation of any state, and is full of mountains. People ski here a lot. There are also old ghost towns, old gold-mining towns, and dude ranches (where guests kind of play cowboy by riding horses, hiking, and having campfires).

Mesa Verde National Park is an ancient Native American town, with houses cut right into the cliffs! The cubbyhole-type houses are colored like the cliffs and high up, almost hidden. Climb into one and imagine what it is like to live as high as an eagle—and to worry about where your next drink of water is coming from.

Colorado is the twenty-sixth largest state in population and has a little more than 4 million people. No one city is much larger than the others, but the capital, Denver, has about 500,000 people, and is the largest.

- Colorado was under Spanish control from the 1500s until 1803. Then the United States bought part of it in the Louisiana Purchase. In 1848 the United States won the Mexican War, and got control of all of Colorado.
- A long stretch of the Continental Divide is also located in Colorado. The Continental Divide is the North American watershed, the point that determines in what direction water flows. On one side of the mountains, all the water in all the rivers flows to the east, toward the Atlantic Ocean. On the other side of the range, it all goes west toward the Pacific.

The West

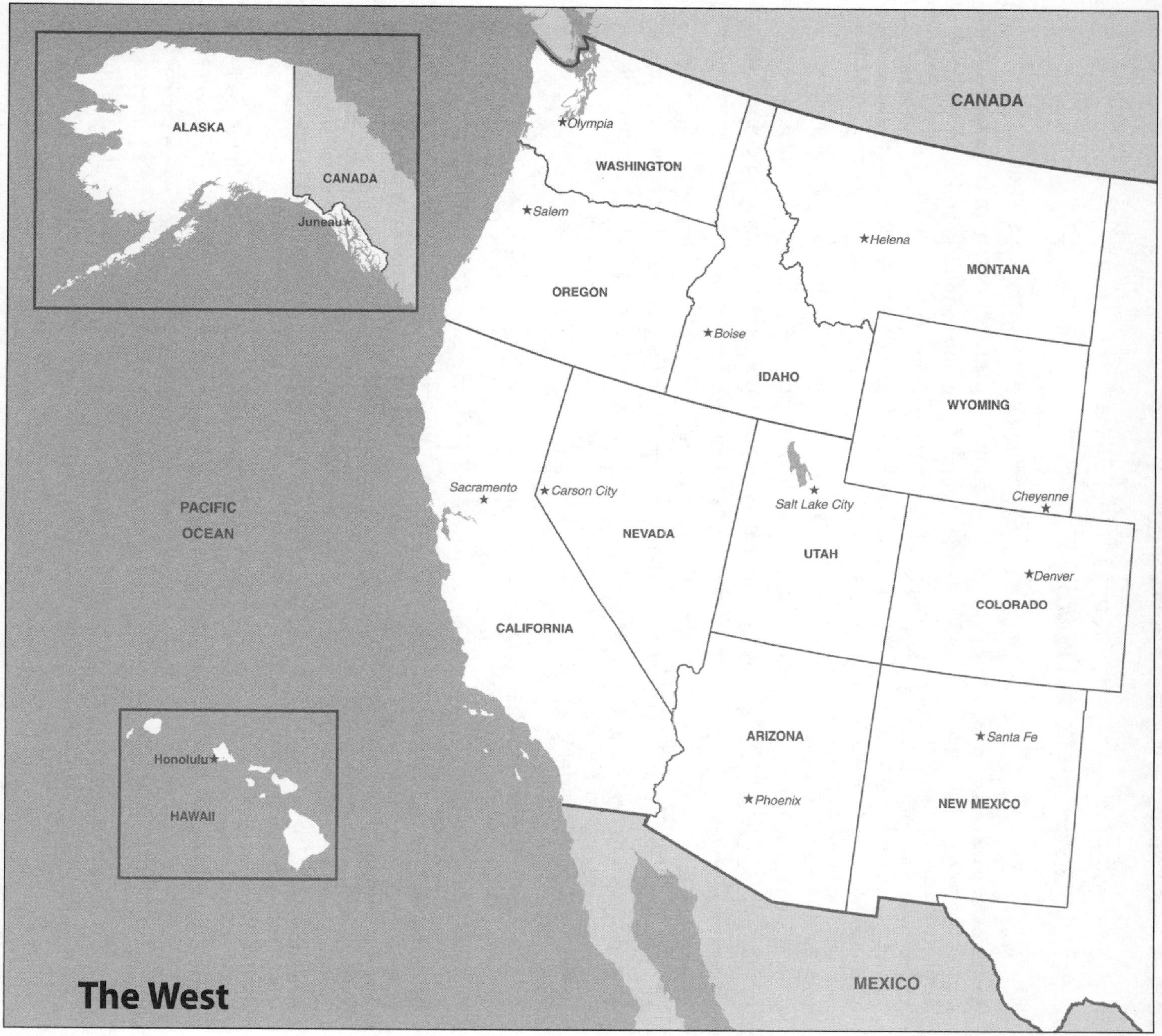

CANADA

MONTANA
★ *Helena*

WYOMING

Cheyenne ★

COLORADO
★ *Denver*

NEW MEXICO
★ *Santa Fe*

MEXICO

IDAHO
★ *Boise*

UTAH
Salt Lake City ★

ARIZONA
★ *Phoenix*

WASHINGTON
★ *Olympia*

OREGON
★ *Salem*

NEVADA
★ *Carson City*

CALIFORNIA
Sacramento ★

CANADA

ALASKA
Juneau ★

PACIFIC
OCEAN

HAWAII
Honolulu ★

Hawaii

Hawaii is the most unusual state in the whole country. A group of five main islands and plenty of smaller ones, Hawaii is located out in the middle of the Pacific Ocean and near the **equator**. These islands came up right out of the ocean and are actually the tops of volcanoes on the ocean's floor. Even though the islands have dirt, grass, waterfalls, birds, huge forests, black sand, and plenty of people, some of the volcanoes are still there—and you can walk right onto two big ones, Kilauea and Mauna Loa.

Hawaii's main islands are Hawaii, Maui, Molokai, Oahu, and Kauai. It's the forty-first largest state in population and has just 1.2 million people. Honolulu is the capital and the largest city.

- In 1941, the Japanese Empire launched an attack on Pearl Harbor. This started the United States' involvement in World War II.
- Once, all the Hawaiian islands were just bare lava rock. Bird droppings mixed with decomposing fish, plants, moss, and living seeds that washed up from the ocean. Some of the seeds sprouted so more plants grew, bringing around more birds and bird droppings. Very, very slowly, this all decayed into a little bit of dirt.
- *equator:* The central "belt" around the fattest part of our planet, the middle. It's not a real belt or a real line, but it divides the earth into the northern and southern hemispheres.

Idaho

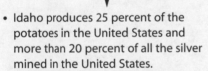

This western state has ghost towns, huge forests, deserts made by old volcanoes, caves, silver mines, rivers with tons of fish, and plenty of mountains. It's also the most famous state for growing potatoes. And there's a place—the Hanford Reservation—where they tested so many nuclear weapons that pollution is a big problem. (You probably don't want to visit there!)

The ghost towns of Custer and Bonanza are in the center of the state, not too far from the Sun Valley ski resort. As with many ghost towns in the west, people just left when they couldn't find any more gold!

Idaho is the forty-second largest state in population and has about 1.3 million people. Boise is the capital and also the largest city in Idaho.

- Idaho produces 25 percent of the potatoes in the United States and more than 20 percent of all the silver mined in the United States.
- Sacajawea, the Indian woman who guided Lewis and Clark as they explored the United States in the early 1800s, was born in Idaho.
- Gold and silver are most often mashed into other, regular rock that isn't worth ten cents. That's called "ore." To mine these minerals, big machines are needed to dig down into the ore, pull it up, and then smash it, to get at the good stuff.

Montana

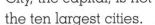 Montana has mountains, giant forests, and deserts, too. The deserts—the dry land of **buttes**, **mesas**, and badlands—are in the northeastern part of the state. Sections of two national parks, Yellowstone (the rest is in Wyoming) and Glacier (the rest is in Canada) are also located in Montana.

This state has very few people, and is one place that has fewer people in the cities than in the rest of the state. Montana is the forty-fourth largest state in population and has just under 900,000 people. Billings is the largest city, with about 92,000 people. Helena, the capital, is the sixth largest city and has just under 29,000 people.

- Eastern Montana is in the rainshadow of the Rocky Mountains. Clouds pile up west of the mountains, which is where the winds come from most often. The clouds get pushed together when they bump into the mountain, the air currents swirl, and the clouds dump their rain. Then they have none left to dump on the places east of the mountains, and that makes eastern Montana dry and desert-like.
- *butte:* A steep and isolated hill.
- *mesa:* A steep and isolated hill or mountain, like a butte, but especially flat on top. The word "mesa" is Spanish for "table."

Nevada

Desert, desert, desert, and Las Vegas—that's Nevada! It also has some cool old western towns, a nuclear testing site (skip that trip!), and part of Death Valley (the rest is in California).

Nevada is the thirty-ninth largest state in population, with about 1.8 million people. Las Vegas is Nevada's largest city and has about 404,000 people. Carson City, the capital, is not even one of the ten largest cities.

- Nevada has been a mining source for gold, silver, lead, and other metals since 1859. Nevada is the driest state in the nation, with some parts receiving less than four inches of rain, per year.
- A state like Nevada that has extinct volcanoes often has gold and silver, too. All those volcanoes churned up the land, from near the surface and also down deep, and the land got very hot from all the lava. The "heavy metals" like gold and silver flow like liquids when they're hot. Then, because they're heavy, they settle down into certain areas. Because they settled in one place, it's easier for us to find them and dig them up later.

New Mexico

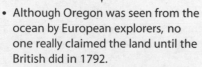 This western state has an ancient, empty Native American "city," Chaco Canyon. It also contains part of the Continental Divide, and plenty of desert.

The Continental Divide starts in Canada, runs through Montana, Wyoming, Colorado, and New Mexico to western Texas and eventually on to the Andes in South America. This "line" is actually the highest point of each of the Rocky Mountains in these states.

New Mexico has just over 1.7 million people, making it the state with the thirty-seventh largest population. Albuquerque, by far the largest city, has about 419,000 people. Santa Fe, the capital, has about 68,000 people.

- The United States gained control of much of the land that is now New Mexico in 1848, after the Mexican War ended. The United States bought the rest, as territory, in 1853.
- Why did the Anasazi Indians abandon Chaco Canyon and their sandstone "apartment" buildings several stories high? No one really knows. It may have been a period of drought (no rain) so severe that with no water, they couldn't continue to live there.

Oregon

This Pacific Northwest state has a dramatic coastline, mountains, volcanoes, a river gorge, ancient lava fields, deep lakes, and even some dry plains.

Overlooking the city of Portland is Mt. Hood, with beautiful trails and lakes. And it's not a hard climb in sneakers. From the top, you can see the highest mountaintops of Washington, the state to the north. These mountains are all old volcanoes, but they are still considered active, including Mt. Hood.

The Columbia River Gorge is also near Portland. An ancient flood, which made the river run ferociously, cut out this dramatic "slash in the ground." Toward the middle of the state is Crater Lake National Park. The lake is in a crater caused when the top of a volcano collapsed into itself because of an eruption.

Oregon is the twenty-ninth largest state in population and has 3.3 million people. Portland is by far the largest city, with about 504,000 people. Salem is the capital and third largest city.

- Although Oregon was seen from the ocean by European explorers, no one really claimed the land until the British did in 1792.
- Today, Oregon produces a lot of lumber and paper, in addition to its large salmon fishing industry.
- How did those giant rocks, called "sea stacks," off the coast get there? They were once just part of the coast itself. The rock that was in between washed away.

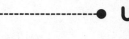

Utah

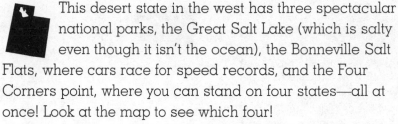 This desert state in the west has three spectacular national parks, the Great Salt Lake (which is salty even though it isn't the ocean), the Bonneville Salt Flats, where cars race for speed records, and the Four Corners point, where you can stand on four states—all at once! Look at the map to see which four!

Bonneville was picked as the best place to get car speed records because it is so flat—and the dried-out salty ground doesn't really have anything to slow a car down. Vrroom!

Utah is the thirty-fifth largest state in population and has a little over 2.1 million people. Salt Lake City, the capital and largest city, has 174,000 people.

- In 1869, Utah was the place where the first railroad to cross the United States came together. Railroad builders started in the east and west, and aimed for the middle. They met—and the railroad tracks came together just right!
- Why is there a salty lake here, nowhere near the ocean? At one time, there was an ocean here; all of it evaporated except for this lake. That's also why there is salt at the Bonneville Salt Flats.

Washington

 This state, in the northwest corner of the continental United States, is the home of the famous volcano Mt. St. Helens. Washington has plenty of dramatic mountains, volcanoes, rivers, rain forests, and coastal areas, along with the most northerly point in the "Lower 48" states (not counting Alaska or Hawaii).

The rain forests of Washington state can be seen nicely in Olympic National Park. Water from the Pacific Ocean cools off very quickly as it starts to hit the mountains. This change in temperature helps to release a ton of rain!

And don't miss Mt. St. Helens Volcanic National Monument. This mountain erupted in 1980, and blew off its northern face entirely. That may seem like a long time ago to you—but for a volcano, it's just yesterday!

Washington is the eighteenth largest state in population and has about 5.8 million people. Seattle is by far the largest city, with about 537,000 people. Olympia, the capital, is not even one of the state's ten largest cities.

- The border between Washington state and the British colony of British Columbia was not settled on until 1846. British Columbia is now a province of Canada.
- What is the Ring of Fire? It's a giant imaginary "ring" in the ocean and near the shore. (Look at a globe, or a map of the Pacific Ocean.) It begins on Alaska's west coast and follows the Pacific Ocean all the way down to the far south tip of South America. Then, it loops out across the Pacific Ocean to the Philippines and up north along the coasts of China, Japan, and Russia, then to Alaska again. Fiery volcanoes and earthquakes occur all along this ring. Washington state is part of this scene!

How do cows travel?
In a moo-ving van!

How does a scaredy-cat travel?
In a yellow cab!

Wyoming

- Wyoming is one of the two states that is almost a perfect square. What is the other one?
- Why does Yellowstone National Park have geysers and boiling mud pits? The crust (the top layer of the earth) is thin here, so hot water and mud can bubble up here more easily. Remember: the farther down you go underground, the hotter it is. The earth's core is a thick stew of bubbling metal!

Wyoming, a Wild West state, includes part of Yellowstone National Park, plenty of Native American sites, desert areas, Grand Tetons National Park, and unusual places such as Devils Tower National Monument and Fossil Butte National Monument.

Fossil Butte National Monument is near Wyoming's southwest corner. This area was actually a lake about 50 million years ago. A lot of animals lived and died around it. Over many years, their bodies were buried deeper and deeper as the lake filled in. These muddy layers later turned to stone, preserving the fossils. You can see fossils of snakes, fish, crocodiles, and birds. And this is a large place with real live cows, deer, moose, and pronghorn antelopes too!

Wyoming has the smallest population of any state, with just under 480,000 people. Cheyenne, the capital and largest city, has about 54,000 people.

Midwest

Illinois

This Midwestern state is part of what is called the U.S. "breadbasket." That means it grows tons of grain for things like flour and cattle feed—not just for the United States, but for many countries around the world.

Chicago, one of the largest cities in the United States, is in Illinois on Lake Michigan. If you've never seen any of the Great Lakes, you may think that—compared to an ocean—they're just ponds. Not so—during storms, Lake Michigan can have waves twenty feet high!

The Mississippi River runs along Illinois' western border. This river used to be almost like an interstate highway, before there were cars. Food, machines, and people—they all moved by river.

Illinois is the sixth largest state in population, with about 12.1 million people. Chicago is the largest city in Illinois and has over 2.8 million people. Springfield is the capital.

• Chicago has many of the United States' first skyscrapers. Several are still there in one piece! In the early days, people thought you had to build the walls of a skyscraper thicker on the first floor than the second, and so on, all the way up. They also didn't build them more than a few floors high—because good elevators hadn't been invented yet.

QUICK QUIZ

Capitals Quiz

Which state capitals have men's first names?

Answer: Pierre (South Dakota), Austin (Texas), Montgomery (Alabama)

Indiana

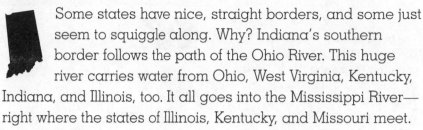

Some states have nice, straight borders, and some just seem to squiggle along. Why? Indiana's southern border follows the path of the Ohio River. This huge river carries water from Ohio, West Virginia, Kentucky, Indiana, and Illinois, too. It all goes into the Mississippi River—right where the states of Illinois, Kentucky, and Missouri meet.

Indianapolis, the capital, is known for its 500 Mile Race that takes place over Memorial Day weekend. The racing cars go more than 200 mph!

Indiana is the fourteenth largest state in population and has about 6 million people. Indianapolis is the capital and is also by far the largest city in population, with 750,000 people.

- Indiana has lots of limestone *quarries*. Limestone is formed from the bodies of ancient sea creatures, so the whole rock is really a fossil.
- In northwestern Indiana, on Lake Michigan, there are huge sand dunes. Small sand dunes are often formed by waves and the wind, but big ones mean that the whole lake was once that level—the dunes were the shoreline.
- *quarry:* A huge hole dug into the ground to get out big pieces of rock.

Iowa

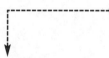

Iowa is bordered on the east by the Mississippi River, and on the west by the Missouri River. On the east, a beautiful stretch of the Mississippi River has cliffs, hills, and hiking trails. In Maquoketa Caves State Park, you can actually climb "inside" these river cliffs.

Iowa has some of the most powerful looking farms you've ever seen—they look almost like factories for corn and more—and many are owned by big corporations.

The Amana Colonies is a cluster of several villages preserved to look like the old farming days. The people here used to speak German, eat their meals together, and share the money when they sold their grain and cows. After awhile, they even started a refrigerator company—Amana Refrigerators.

Iowa is the thirtieth largest state in population, with just over 2.8 million people. Des Moines is the capital and the largest city, just a little bit larger than Cedar Rapids and Davenport.

- The land that is now Iowa was first bought from the French in 1803. It was part of the Louisiana Purchase.
- Iowa has very high-quality soil for farming, and a huge number of small and medium-sized rivers. These two facts are actually related. Over thousands of years, the rivers have moved around a bit and have left oozy river muck behind. This muck dried out long ago, and the decomposed plants and animals made the rich soil.

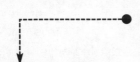

Kansas

Kansas is known for its dramatic weather. It was pounded, once, by the largest hailstones ever weighed—1.67 pounds apiece! It is also in the string of states—Kansas, Oklahoma, and Texas—that gets blasted by one-third of all the tornadoes that hit North America. Remember Dorothy and Toto from *The Wizard of Oz*? They were from Kansas!

Kansas is partly "Old West." It has part of the Santa Fe Trail, nine miles west of Dodge City. Pioneers used the trail to go west, and ranchers used it to herd cattle. Stagecoaches, freight wagons, and soldiers used it, too. Some wagon wheel ruts are still there.

Kansas is the thirty-second largest state in population and has just over 2.6 million people. Topeka, the capital, is the fourth largest city and has about 119,000 people.

- The geographic center of the continental United States (not counting Alaska and Hawaii) is near the town of Lebanon, Kansas, in Smith County.
- Bison—also called buffalo—were once very common in Kansas. And they are getting to be again. They don't get cold outside in the winter. Their big hoofs can paw right through deep snow to find grasses to eat.

Michigan

Michigan is a Great Lakes state. The lower, larger part of the state is bordered by Lake Michigan on its west side, Lake Huron on most of its east side, and Lake Erie along its southeast corner (by Detroit). Michigan also has an Upper Peninsula, another chunk of the state. This part has Lake Michigan on its south side and Lake Superior to the north. The very eastern part of the UP touches Canada and is just a few miles from Lake Ontario.

Sleeping Bear Dunes National Lakeshore is in the north-western part of the Lower Peninsula. You can drive a seven- to eight-mile road and see giant piles of sand, then two islands out in the big lake. There is a nine-mile hiking trail, too.

Michigan has the eighth largest population, with about 9.9 million people. Lansing is the capital, but Detroit, the Motor City, is the largest city.

- In northern Michigan, at the Straits of Mackinac, Lake Michigan and Lake Huron come together. The Mackinac Bridge over the straits covers 5 miles from the Lower Peninsula to the Upper Peninsula. It's called a "suspension bridge" because the roadway is held up (suspended) by thick metal cables attached to very high posts that are buried deep into the rock under the water.

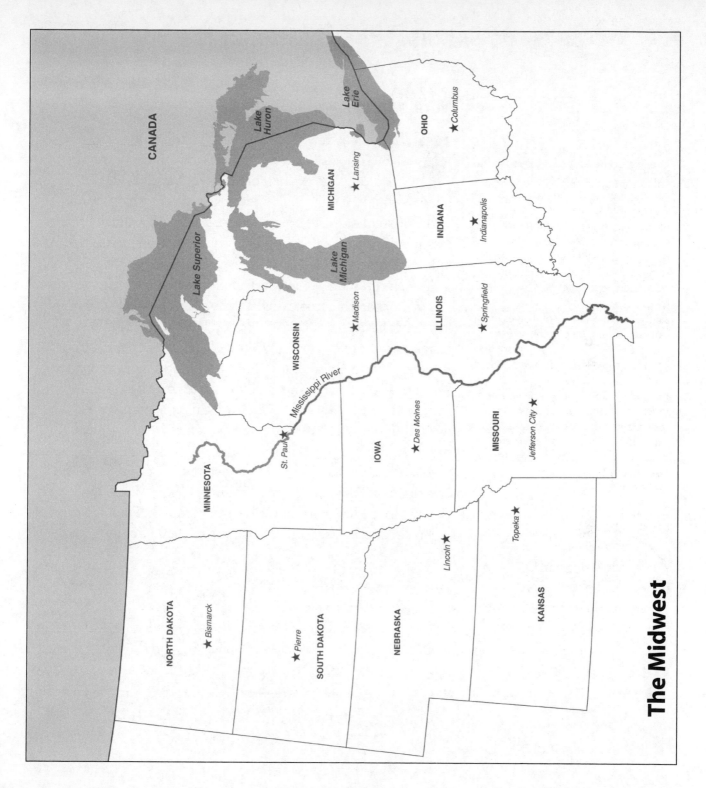

CANADA

Lake Huron

Lake Erie

OHIO
★ *Columbus*

Lake Superior

MICHIGAN
★ *Lansing*

INDIANA
★ *Indianapolis*

Lake Michigan

WISCONSIN
★ *Madison*

ILLINOIS
★ *Springfield*

Mississippi River

IOWA
★ *Des Moines*

MISSOURI
★ *Jefferson City*

★ *St. Paul*

MINNESOTA

KANSAS
★ *Topeka*

NEBRASKA
★ *Lincoln*

NORTH DAKOTA
★ *Bismarck*

SOUTH DAKOTA
★ *Pierre*

The Midwest

Minnesota

Minnesota is another Great Lakes State. Lake Superior's North Shore is along the northeastern border. The license plate says "Land of 10,000 Lakes"—but that only counts the lakes that are bigger than 10 acres. If smaller lakes counted, there would be many times that number. The source of the Mississippi River is also located in Minnesota.

The North Shore, between Duluth and the Canadian border, is a wilderness of forests, cliffs, waterfalls, smaller lakes, and the black beaches of Lake Superior. Duluth is a big port city, reachable by ships from anywhere. The ships come in from the Atlantic Ocean, through the St. Lawrence Seaway, which looks like a river on a map. The St. Lawrence starts between New Brunswick and Quebec, in Canada. Ships continue west through four of the five Great Lakes before arriving in Duluth, at the western end of Lake Superior.

Minnesota is the twentieth largest state in population and has about 4.8 million people. The Twin Cities, Minneapolis and St. Paul, are Minnesota's two largest cities. St. Paul, the capital, is the second largest and has about 257,000 people.

- The first Europeans to discover Minnesota were the French, but it came under U.S. control by 1818.
- Parts of Minnesota used to be covered by **glaciers.** As the glaciers moved across the state, getting bigger and smaller, and bigger again, they scraped out areas. These areas later filled with water and became lakes.
- Minnesota has plenty of wolves in its northern area, deep in the forests. Like many wild animals, they don't bother people if people don't bother them.
- *glacier:* A large, slow-moving body of ice that either comes down from mountains, or spreads outward. Currently, most glaciers are in the polar regions, around the North and South poles.

How does an IRS collector travel?
In a tax-i!

How does a football team travel?
By coach!

Pretty Postcards

Sonja is driving with her family from your home in Maine back to her house in California. On the way she stops in eighteen different states. At each stop she mails you a postcard with the state abbreviation on it. But the postcards don't arrive at your house in order! See if you can plot Sonja's trip on the map below. Shade in each state as you put the postcards in order from Maine to California.

I hope my **CA**+ isn't fat Sonja	We're still o**KY** Dokey Sonja	It's just **ME** Sonja
It's still cold up **N**o**RT**H Sonja	we are **OK**! Sonja	The dog eats s**TX**! WEIRD DOG. Sonja
This trip was a good **ID**ea Sonja	We sure **LA**UGH a lot! Sonja	I sure **MIS**s you lots!! Sonja
We **NV**R went to your school! Sonja	My **PA** says "Hi" Sonja	we **WAVE** to trucks Sonja
HUGS & **KIS**ses Sonja	My **MA** says "Hi" Sonja	I need a **NE**w pencil. Sonja
We don't have a **NY** bubblegum Sonja	I saw **TN** deer today! Sonja	**WY** don't you visit me next time? Sonja

Missouri

Missouri is bounded on the east by the Mississippi River, where the river is wide and powerful. Just imagine Huck Finn, Tom Sawyer, and Jim out there on a raft—like in the books *The Adventures of Tom Sawyer* and *Huckleberry Finn*. Those famous books were written by Mark Twain, who was once a steamboat pilot on the river.

St. Louis, known as The Gateway to the West, was the starting point for explorers Lewis and Clark, who charted the Louisiana Purchase in 1804. The Gateway Arch is a monument to the start of the Santa Fe and Oregon trails, the Pony Express, and a city that was an important trading center between the east and the west during the 1800s.

Missouri is the fifteenth largest state in population and has almost 5.5 million people. Kansas City is the largest city, with almost 442,000 people. Jefferson City, the capital, isn't even among the top ten in size.

- Missouri was more or less ruled by the French from 1682 to 1803. Then the United States bought Missouri in the Louisiana Purchase of 1803. Missouri stayed in the Union during the Civil War, but a very large number of people sided with the south.
- Why are the banks of the Mississippi River so high? The river itself cut the "canyon" it runs through now. Over millions of years, it has washed away rock and more rock, so the water level is slowly getting lower and lower.

Nebraska

Nebraska has an interesting personality. The eastern half seems like a state in the Midwest, but emptier. The western half is definitely "western," a cowboy country of prairie grasslands and buffalo. What makes the difference? Rainfall. Without enough rain in western Nebraska, farming doesn't work well, so the people have started ranching.

In pioneer days, many families going west came through Nebraska by a place called Scottsbluff. As the pioneers came across the prairie in their Conestoga (covered) wagons, they could see the bluff from many miles away. That's how they knew they were going in the right direction! Scottsbluff became part

- In the early 1800s, Lewis and Clark explored Nebraska. Soon after that, it became the starting point for the first **transcontinental** railroad.
- How did Nebraska get its Sand Hills? Long ago, there was ocean west of here. (Remember that the continents moved around and so did the oceans.) As it dried up, it left a lot of sand. Then wind blew it over here!
- ***transcontinental:*** Across the continent. The prefix "trans" usually means across or beyond.

of the Oregon Trail (one of the routes west before there were any highways or any cars). Now, we can even drive up the bluff.

Nebraska is the thirty-sixth largest state in population and has about 1.7 million people. Omaha, the largest city, has about 372,000 people. Lincoln, the capital and second largest city, has 213,000 people.

North Dakota

Part of the Great Plains, North Dakota has **badlands**, old Indian villages, a pioneer village, and lots of emptiness.

Badlands are only bad if you're having trouble in them. The pioneers, in covered wagons, did! To us now, badlands are astounding shapes, layers, colors, and sizes of rock formations. In the Theodore Roosevelt National Memorial Park, North Unit, you can see where Teddy Roosevelt hunted buffalo in the badlands before he became president.

The Geographical Center Pioneer Village and Museum, near Rugby, is at the exact geographic center of the whole North American continent (the United States, Canada, Mexico, and Central America). From here, it is about 1,500 miles to all the oceans, Atlantic, Pacific, and Arctic. There is also a restored pioneer town.

North Dakota has the forty-seventh largest population, with 634,000 people. Fargo is the largest city, with about 87,000 people. Bismarck, the capital, has almost 54,000 people.

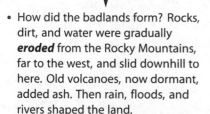

- How did the badlands form? Rocks, dirt, and water were gradually *eroded* from the Rocky Mountains, far to the west, and slid downhill to here. Old volcanoes, now dormant, added ash. Then rain, floods, and rivers shaped the land.
- *badlands:* Region of high hills with many colorful rock layers and jagged edges.
- *erode:* To slowly wear, or wash away. Hurricanes and ocean storms have eroded many beaches, due to strong winds and rough seas.

Ohio

This Midwestern state is the birthplace of two presidents, and the home of some natural wonders, too. One is an island with huge "claw marks" made by a glacier.

The glacier "claw marks" are on Kelleys Island in Lake Erie. To get to the island, you take a short ferry ride out from the town of Marblehead. Glaciers are heavy with ice and rocks that make deep scratches as they go over other big rocks. On Kelleys Island, the marks are several inches up to ten to fifteen feet deep and up to thirty feet wide!

Near (but not on) Route 90 are the Seneca Caverns, which were discovered by two boys and a dog—they fell into its opening! Later it was explored, and it goes down seven different levels. A tour there takes you through some of it.

Ohio is the seventh largest state in population and has about 11.3 million people. Columbus, the capital and largest city, has about 670,000 people. Cleveland, the second largest city, has almost 500,000 people.

- President James Garfield's National Historic Site is in Mentor. He ran for President in 1880, got elected, and was assassinated only a few months later. You can tour his house.
- President Ulysses Grant was born near the town of New Richmond. His birthplace can also be toured.
- How are caves formed? Most are made when underground rivers cut through soft rock, such as limestone. The Seneca Caverns were made by a huge fracture, or cut, in the limestone, and there is a river here now.

South Dakota

Buffalo, a Laura Ingalls Wilder house, and two wildly different national parks make this Great Plains state very interesting. Do you like the *Little House on the Prairie* books? The town of De Smet has one of Laura's real houses, one of her parents' houses, a church that "Pa" helped to build, and a lot more to tour!

Wind Cave National Park has 40 miles of passageways and quite a few underground tours. One is done in the dark, by candlelight. Badlands National Park has no caves. Instead, it looks as though a giant grabbed a bunch of clay and made some strange

- Settlers discovered gold in the state's Black Hills in 1874, and South Dakota is still the second largest producer of gold in the United States.
- Why does South Dakota have so many caves? Like Indiana and Ohio, South Dakota has a lot of limestone. Limestone is soft (for a rock) and crumbles easily. As streams and rivers flow underground, they carve out caves.

shapes. You can climb up and around these dry hills, flat-topped blobs, and pointy ridges that look like the skyline of a city.

South Dakota is the forty-fifth largest state in population and has about 733,000 people. Sioux Falls is by far the largest city, with 117,000 people, but the capital is Pierre.

Wisconsin

Like Minnesota, this is a state for water fun. The glaciers left tons of lakes, including parts of Lake Superior and Lake Michigan that border Wisconsin. It's also a state of cows, cows, and more cows. Dairy farming leads to cheese production. That's why you can call Wisconsin people "cheese heads"!

In Lake Superior, Madeline Island is a half-hour ferryboat trip out. You can bike, hike, walk the beaches, and climb the dunes. Or, if you prefer the city, you can go to Milwaukee, home of the Harley-Davidson Motor Company, famous for their American-made motorcycles. Milwaukee is also very well known for beer, including Pabst and Miller.

Wisconsin is the sixteenth largest state in population and has just under 5.3 million people. Milwaukee is by far the largest city and has just about 578,000 people. Madison, the capital and second largest city, has about 209,000 people.

- Even though the Revolutionary War had ended long ago, Great Britain didn't give up control of Wisconsin until after the War of 1812.
- What water runs along Wisconsin's western side? The Mississippi River. This powerful river has cut out its own channel over thousands and thousands of years. That's what makes all the bluffs and cliffs. The river once ran right along their tops.

QUICK QUIZ

Capitals Quiz

What capitals are women's names?

Answer: Helena (Montana), Olympia (Washington), Cheyenne (Wyoming), and Madison (Wisconsin)

South

Alabama

This deep south state has a very small coastline on the Gulf of Mexico. But Mobile, Alabama, is a very old **port city** for huge ships from the Atlantic Ocean.

A bit farther south from Mobile is Gulf State Park. For ocean fun, you can walk out a long fishing pier or take a trail called "Alligator Trail." (Guess why?) At the tip of this small peninsula is a fort (Fort Gaines) with another fort (Fort Morgan) across the water. A ferryboat connects them.

Alabama is the twenty-second largest state in population, with about 4.4 million people. Birmingham is Alabama's largest city, with about 250,000 people. The state's capital, Montgomery, is the third largest city.

- Alabama was important in the Civil Rights movement during the 1950s and 1960s. There were protests in Montgomery, Alabama, to end *segregation,* as well as a big march in Selma, Alabama.
- Alligators live in Alabama, too—lots of them! You might be able to go on an alligator safari, and take a boat through the swamps and lakes where they live. Keep your eyes open, though—alligators can also live in marshes and even drainage canals.
- *port city:* A city on an ocean, large lake, or river, with big docks, buoys, and all the equipment that large ships need to load and unload their cargo. Many very old and well-known cities around the world are located on the water because that's where international trading ships landed.
- *segregation:* Forced separation. The Civil Rights movement had many goals, but one was to end the forced separation of black and white people in schools, restaurants, churches, and buses—everywhere!

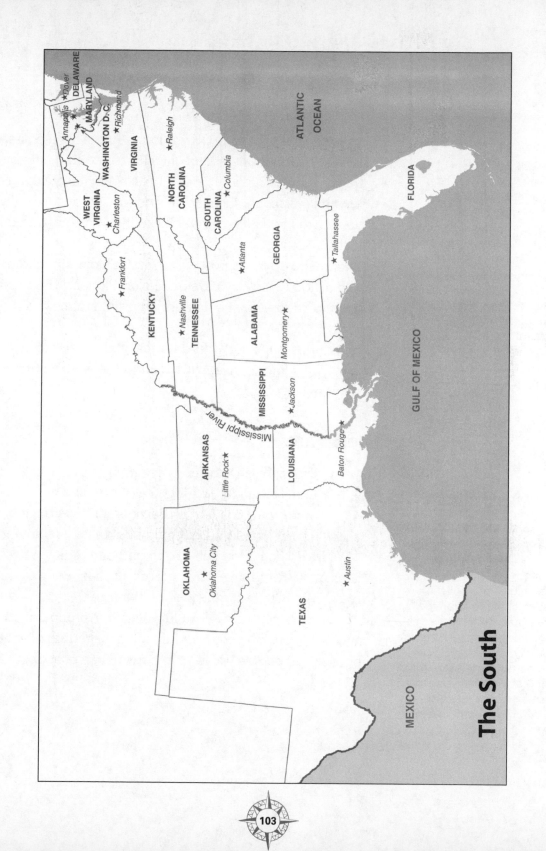

The South

Arkansas

- The forty-second President of the United States, William Jefferson Clinton, was governor of Arkansas before he was president.
- The Mississippi River is one of the United States' three most important "flyways." That means that lots of birds fly over it as they migrate north in the springtime and south in the fall. The birds use the river as a guide to stay on course, and as a source of water and stuff to eat.

The Mississippi River forms Arkansas's eastern border. The states of Oklahoma and a little bit of Texas are to its west. To its south is Louisiana and to its north is Missouri. Just like its location, Arkansas really is a little bit like the south, a little bit like the Midwest, and a little bit like the west.

Arkansas also has part of the Ozark Mountain chain. Part of the range has a cave system called Blanchard Springs Caverns. These are spectacular caves that almost no one has heard of!

Arkansas is the thirty-third largest state in population, with about 2.5 million people. Little Rock is the state's capital and the largest city.

Delaware

- Delaware was governed by the Netherlands and Sweden before finally coming under English control in 1664. In 1787 it became the first state to ratify (agree to) the U.S. Constitution.
- Find a "tide table" on a bulletin board at one of the parks on the beach. This chart shows when the tide is high (farthest up on the shore) and when it is low. Did you know that the moon's gravity makes the tides? Think of the oceans as a loose blue sweater worn by the earth—as the moon orbits the earth, it gently pulls the water with it.

Not only is Delaware very small, but at its narrowest part, around Middletown, it's only about 35 miles across. From its northwest corner you can see Pennsylvania and Maryland at the same time.

Delaware has a long shoreline and one really big city, Wilmington. There are lots of great beaches. Bombay Hook National Wildlife Refuge is one of them.

Delaware is the forty-sixth largest state in population, with only about 750,000 people. Wilmington is the largest city with about 72,000 people. Dover, the capital, has only about 36,000.

District of Columbia

The U.S. capital is filled with important government buildings and monuments. It has the Capitol, the Lincoln and Jefferson memorials, the Washington Monument, and the White House. You can see the real Declaration of Independence at the National Archives, you can watch them making money at the U.S. Mint, and you can see space capsules at the Smithsonian Air and Space Museum. And that's just a start!

Washington, D.C., is not a state, is the twenty-third largest city in the United States, and has about 523,000 people. It's not a big area on the map—D.C. is only about 68 square miles.

- In 1790, the U.S. Congress set aside some land along the Potomac River to be used for a new capital. The land came out of both Virginia and Maryland. In 1846, the Virginia part was returned to Virginia. But the part from Maryland was still big enough for the capital.
- In the 1970s and early 1980s, people tried to get Washington, D.C., to be treated more like a state, with a senator and a representative. But so far this hasn't happened—D.C. has one representative in Congress, but that person can't vote on any laws.

Florida

Orlando, Florida, has the biggest bunch of theme parks all in one place in the whole world! But there are lots of other exciting places in Florida, too. Cape Canaveral is where NASA launches the space shuttle and rockets. Near the shuttle launch pad is the Merritt Island National Wildlife Refuge. Do you think the noise of the shuttle scares the alligators and beautiful white egrets, birds with long necks?

Florida also has the Everglades National Park. They have alligator boat tours, some of them at night. And you can drive through the park between Naples and Miami. Look for cool birds, lots of swampland, and maybe wild orchids.

Florida is the fourth largest state in population and has about 15 million people. Tallahassee, the capital, is the state's eighth largest city.

- Florida is called the Sunshine State. The climate is perfect for agricultural products, including oranges, grapefruits, melons, strawberries, and sugar cane.
- The Florida **Keys** started out as living coral reefs. Over time, birds, plants, and animals slowly turned the exposed reefs into land, like Hawaii. Now, some of the keys have roads, motels, docks, and homes.
- *key:* A low island or reef.

Georgia

- Georgia was part of the Confederacy, the southern states that fought during the Civil War. General Sherman, from the Union army (the northern states), burned Atlanta in 1864 during this war. He also destroyed the land all the way to Savannah.
- *barrier island:* An island close to the shore that comes between the ocean and the land. There are lots of them along the Atlantic coast, especially in North Carolina, South Carolina, and Georgia. They are usually just sandbars, and so they sometimes move when there's a big hurricane. Small ones can even get completely washed away.

Georgia is an interesting blend of modern America and "Old South" tradition. Atlanta, the capital, is both modern and traditional. The world headquarters of Coca-Cola is in Atlanta, and the 1996 Summer Olympics were held there.

Savannah is a very old city, on the coast near South Carolina's southeast corner. The city has big old southern houses built around grassy squares, and an area near the Savannah River is fixed up to look like the old days.

On the road between Savannah and the northeast corner of Florida are a lot of **barrier islands**. The two most wonderful ones are probably Sapelo Island and Cumberland Island, but you have to take a ferry boat to get to them.

Georgia is the eleventh most populated state, and its population is almost 8 million.

Heading Home

You have finished your vacation at the beach—now it's time to return home. Start at the word SEA. Travel one space at a time making compound words as you go until reaching the word HOME. You can move up and down, and side to side, but not diagonally!

START SEA	SHELL	FISH	HOOK
HORSE	BACK	HAND	BALL
FLY	YARD	OUT	GAME
PAPER	STICK	BREAK	DOWN
BACK	FIRE	FAST	TOWN FINISH

Kentucky

Hodgenville, Kentucky, has the first memorial to Honest Abe. They have moved the log cabin where he was born inside another building, to keep it from falling apart. Lincoln is noted for enacting the Emancipation Proclamation, and delivering the Gettysburg Address in 1863. He was assassinated on April 14, 1865.

Kentucky is best known for horse farms and racing. The Kentucky Derby is a horserace held at Churchill Downs every year. The racetrack has a museum dedicated to champion horses and the history of horse racing in the area.

Kentucky is the twenty-third largest state in population, with almost four million people. The largest city, Louisville, is ten times bigger (253,000) than the capital, Frankfort.

- During the Civil War, Kentucky had both Union and Confederate soldiers, and sometimes two brothers in one family were fighting in the war on separate sides.
- Can you be "blind as a shrimp"? Yes. Mammoth Cave is so dark that several species of creatures have become blind. They couldn't see anything if they could see! It happened this way: seeing stuff didn't give any shrimp any advantage—it was just too dark. So, after millions of years, sight just sort of dropped out of their genes.

Louisiana

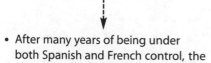

Louisiana is an Old South state, with old plantations huge gardens, and amazing swamps. The Mississippi River pours into the Gulf of Mexico in southern Louisiana. The river is so large and powerful that it sloshes over the land, moves sandbars, and makes islands. If you look at a detailed map of Louisiana's coastline, you'll almost wonder whether some of those places are land or water. They are both—and called a "bayou."

Houma, a town on the south coast, is a great place to take a swamp tour in a boat. Yes, you will see alligators—also cypress trees dressed in moss, egrets, and more.

Louisiana is the twenty-first largest state in population and has almost 4.4 million people. New Orleans, the state's largest city, has about 470,000 people, more than twice the size of Baton Rouge, the capital.

- After many years of being under both Spanish and French control, the land that is now Louisiana was sold in 1803 to the United States as a part of the Louisiana Purchase.
- Alligators look basically the same today as they did 100 million years ago. Alligators (like the cockroach, some beetles, some sharks, and others) are so well adapted to where they live that they haven't had to evolve or change much.

Maryland

 In addition to having many suburbs for Washington, D.C., Maryland also has Chesapeake Bay, a very large inlet of the Atlantic Ocean.

Chesapeake Bay is famous for its crabs, and in many of the towns you can see the fishing boats. This bay also has 8,000 miles of shoreline! That's more miles than the length of the United States from east to west. The bay's shoreline has so many points and peninsulas that by the time you'd walked along all that beach, you'd be up to 8,000 miles.

Maryland is the nineteenth largest state in population and has just under 5.2 million people. Maryland's largest city is Baltimore, and Annapolis is its capital.

- The area that is now Maryland was once the territory of some of North America's most ancient Native American civilizations. Some of them existed more than 12,000 years ago.
- In the War of 1812, British troops tried to take the city of Baltimore. Their assault on Fort McHenry, in Baltimore's harbor, led Francis Scott Key to compose the words to "The Star Spangled Banner."
- What are those huge piles of sticks you see high up on old docks? Osprey nests. The osprey is a **raptor** and it hunts fish in the sea.
- *raptor:* A hunting bird with claws for grabbing prey.

Mississippi

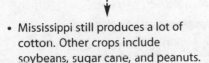 In Greenwood, see the Florewood River Plantation. It is restored to be as it was in the 1850s, prior to the Civil War. In the fall, visitors may pick some cotton in the field—think about how hard that life was for plantation laborers (most of whom were slaves). And in Vicksburg, you can tour a Civil War battlefield. Some of the cannons are still there.

Mississippi is the thirty-first largest state in population and has about 2.8 million people. Jackson, the state's capital and largest city, has a little over 188,000 people.

- Mississippi still produces a lot of cotton. Other crops include soybeans, sugar cane, and peanuts.
- Trees draped with moss are a common site in this state. This moss is a plant, but it is not attached to the ground. It lives by capturing sunlight and rain right where it is, hanging on the tree.

North Carolina

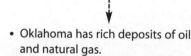

- North Carolina was one of the thirteen original U.S. colonies, and was first settled by English settlers in 1653.

North Carolina has a lovely section of the Blue Ridge Mountains, and part of the Smoky Mountains, which is part of the Appalachians. It also has Kitty Hawk, and the Outer Banks with many islands.

The Blue Ridge Mountains Parkway is in the far western part of North Carolina. This line of very old mountains (now just really high hills) is blue when seen from a distance.

On the opposite side of the state is Kitty Hawk, where the Wright brothers flew the first airplane in the world. It was a simple glider with no walls to keep out the wind.

North Carolina is the tenth largest state in population and has just under 7.7 million people. Charlotte is by far the largest city, with a population of 505,000 people. Charlotte is almost twice the size of Raleigh, the second largest city and the capital.

Oklahoma

- Oklahoma has rich deposits of oil and natural gas.

Like Western states, Oklahoma has neat pioneer sites and Native American sites. It also has mountains, dry grasslands, oil wells, and an unusual shape.

Near Aline is a Homesteader's sod house. There wasn't enough wood on the prairies for pioneer families to make roofs. Trees made the houses' framework, and sod (strips of grass and dirt) was plastered down with clay for roofs.

"Sequoyah's House" is near the town of Sallisaw. Here, a man named George Guess (also called Sequoyah) created the alphabet (with 86 letters!) for the Cherokee Indian language. They had never written anything down before.

Oklahoma has the twenty-eighth largest population, with about 3.4 million people. Oklahoma City, the capital and largest city, has about 472,000 people.

South Carolina

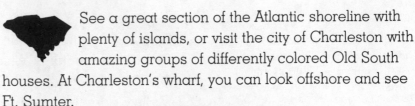

See a great section of the Atlantic shoreline with plenty of islands, or visit the city of Charleston with amazing groups of differently colored Old South houses. At Charleston's wharf, you can look offshore and see Ft. Sumter.

Kiawah Island, not far from Charleston, has houses but also lots of nature. The beach sand is hard enough to ride bikes on easily. There are nature trails through the woods, and plenty of alligators. You can't outrun them, so don't get close!

South Carolina is the twenty-fifth most populated state, with a population of 3.9 million. Columbia, the capital and largest city, has about 111,000 people. Charleston, the second largest city, has 87,000 people.

- Ft. Sumter is the place the Civil War began in 1861. South Carolina soldiers fired at it. They were the first state to **secede** from the union.
- Why does South Carolina have so many hurricanes? All the southern states on the Atlantic Ocean do. Hurricanes happen when the ocean is lots warmer than the air. As warm air rises up from the ocean and hits colder air, it can swirl and swirl faster. This can make giant areas of clouds like big wheels. They spit out tons of rain and have winds that can knock over buildings.
- *secede:* For one thing to separate itself from a group or organization. During the Civil War, several states seceded from the United States (the Union) to form their own group (the Confederacy).

Tennessee

The most visited areas in Tennessee are probably the Great Smoky Mountains National Park on the eastern border, and the city of Nashville, for its country music scene. But it also has a restored Native American village, mountains, and the giant Tennessee River Valley.

Near Memphis, at Chucalissa, is a Choctaw Indian town that was probably abandoned as long ago as the 1500s. There are plenty of Indian houses and a burial mound—with skeletons!

Tennessee is the seventeenth most populous state and has just under 5.5 million people. Memphis is the largest city and has about 604,000 people. Nashville, the capital, is part of a two-city area with 510,000 people.

- The states that border Tennessee are: North Carolina, Georgia, Alabama, Mississippi, Arkansas, Missouri, Kentucky, and Virginia. That's eight! Can any state beat this record?
- Why are the Smoky Mountains smoky? It's air pollution!
- Memphis is also home to the monument of a world-famous man—some might call him the King—Elvis Presley's Graceland.

Texas

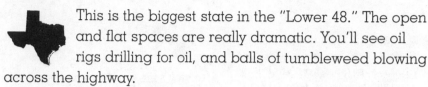

This is the biggest state in the "Lower 48." The open and flat spaces are really dramatic. You'll see oil rigs drilling for oil, and balls of tumbleweed blowing across the highway.

Big Bend National Park and Padre Island National Seashore are two really cool places. Big Bend is a river in the south-western part of the state. And Padre Island is in the eastern part, in the Gulf of Mexico—check for hurricane warnings first!

Texas is the third largest state in population and has about 20 million people. Houston is the largest city and has about 1.8 million people. Austin, the capital, has about 552,000 people.

- Texas was first under Spanish control, then Mexican. The United States gained control in the mid-1800s.
- Texans Lyndon B. Johnson and George W. Bush became U.S. presidents.
- Did you know that when geologists and oil companies drill for oil, they find all gooped up with sand or rock. It takes real science to figure out how to get it out, separate it from the sand or rock, then transport it in pipelines to a **refinery** before it's gasoline or heating oil.
- *refinery:* The building and equipment used to get the impurities out of something. Oil, sugar, and metal need to be processed in a refinery before they can be used.

Virginia

Like Maryland, Virginia has many suburbs of Washington, D.C. It also has a huge swath of the Blue Ridge Mountains, the restored colonial town of Williamsburg, and Jamestown, where some of the first set-tlers came to America from England.

In Colonial Williamsburg, you can walk through a wig shop, a tavern, and the Governor's palace. And everyone who works here dresses up as though it were the late 1600s or early 1700s. Jamestown is impressive, too. You can see parts of the real houses the settlers built. What would it have been like to be the first people from Europe to come to America?

Virginia is the twelfth largest state in population and has almost 6.9 million people. Virginia Beach, the largest city, has a little over 432,000 people. Richmond, the capital, has about 194,000 people.

- Former U.S. presidents Harrison, Jefferson, Madison, Monroe, Taylor, Tyler, Washington, and Wilson were *all* born in Virginia.
- What three early Presidents have houses in Virginia that can be visited? Thomas Jefferson's Monticello outside Charlottesville, George Washington's Mount Vernon, and James Madison's Montpelier (near Charlottesville).

West Virginia

This oddly shaped state is very mountainous. The mountains are part of the Appalachian range, which runs from Maine all the way to Alabama. Most states give their part of these mountains an additional name because long ago no one knew that it was all one range. In West Virginia, the mountains are called the Highlands.

West Virginia has its Monongahela National Forest, a giant area with plenty of black bears. Remember, they're not like grizzlies. Black bears don't want to bother people unless those people bother them.

West Virginia is the thirty-fourth largest state in population and has just over 1.8 million people. Charleston, the capital and largest city, has about 55,000 people.

- West Virginia was once part of Virginia. The land that is now West Virginia separated from Virginia during the Civil War, after Virginia had already seceded from the Union (United States).
- Today, West Virginia is a big coal producer, turning out about 15 percent of the United States' total. About three-quarters of West Virginia is forests.
- At the National Radio Astronomy Observatory, in Green Bank, scientists study the radio waves of the universe. Radio waves studied in astronomy are a kind of radiation that an object like a star gives off. The telescope at this observatory is 100 yards in diameter—that's the length of a football field!

Cross-Country Chuckles

Here are the names of six states. Put them in the correct blanks to make three silly state riddles.

HINT: The pictures will give you a clue!

NEW JERSEY
TENNESSEE
DELAWARE
MARYLAND
ARKANSAS
IDAHO

What did
_____?
She wore her
_____!

What did
_____?
She saw what
_____!

What did
_____?
She hoed her
_____!

Northeast

Connecticut

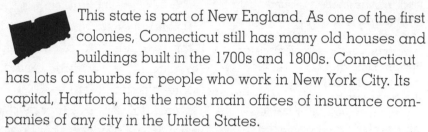 This state is part of New England. As one of the first colonies, Connecticut still has many old houses and buildings built in the 1700s and 1800s. Connecticut has lots of suburbs for people who work in New York City. Its capital, Hartford, has the most main offices of insurance companies of any city in the United States.

Yale University is in New Haven. Lois' Lunch was supposedly the first restaurant in America to sell hamburgers—back in 1900!

Connecticut has the fifth highest population density. That means there are a lot of people living in a pretty small state.

- Connecticut was the main builder of guns and cannons during the Revolutionary War.
- Two-hundred and fifty miles of shoreline on Long Island Sound and many inland lakes make Connecticut a big resort state, too. What is the Long Island Sound? It is just part of the ocean between Connecticut and called Long Island, which is part of New York state.
- Suburbs are the fastest growing living area in the United States. More than 35 percent of Americans now live in suburbs.

Maine

In the northeastern corner of the United States, you'll find "Vacationland." This state of moose, forest, ocean beaches, islands, seals, and more is known for camps and camping. The first place in the United States that the sun shines on every morning, as the earth turns, is Mt. Katahdin, Maine. And West Quoddy Head, a peninsula pointing east, is the most easterly place in the United States. There is a very nice state park in Quoddy Head, with views of the peninsula.

Maine's ocean shore has plenty of lighthouses. Moose Peak Lighthouse is one of the two foggiest places in the United States. (The other one is out west, in Washington.)

Maine is the thirty-eighth largest state in population and has just over 1.2 million people. Portland is the largest city but still has only about 63,000 people. The state's capital, Augusta, has 20,000 people.

- Maine was the state where the Revolutionary War essentially began. American colonists took control of a British ship off the coast of Maine. Then British soldiers burned down the city that is now Portland.
- The seals of Maine are well adapted to cold ocean water, with a thick layer of blubber, and lungs that let them dive down deep.
- Moose are cool, but don't get close—they chaaaaarge! You'd have to climb a tree fast to get away—but even 6 feet high up in a tree isn't even higher than a moose's antlers. Moose usually kick their hoofs for defense, but they don't bother people, unless people bother them.

Massachusetts

 Many events of the American Revolution—the war that turned a bunch of English colonies into an independent country—happened in Massachusetts. The Freedom Trail in Boston is a 2-mile walking tour of some of the important places in early American history. Many buildings, cemeteries, and even an old battleship are still here.

Massachusetts is a coastal state. You can go on a whale watch from the cool New England Aquarium, or take a boat all the way out to Provincetown at the tip of Cape Cod. On the way through the harbor, you see some small islands in one direction—and the skyline of Boston in the other.

Massachusetts is the thirteenth largest state in population, with just under 6.2 million people. Boston is the capital and the most populous city, with about 560,000 people.

- The Pilgrims landed on Plymouth Rock in Massachusetts, founding the Plymouth Colony in 1620.
- The Boston Tea Party, a protest against British taxes, took place in Boston Harbor in 1773.
- Cape Cod, the part of Massachusetts that sticks into the ocean like an arm, was named after codfish. There are still lots of fish there near a reef called George's Bank—the whales feed on them, and that's why the whale-watching boats go out to this historic fishing place.

New Hampshire

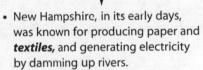 Do you know what a "leaf-peeper" is? It is not an insect and not a bird. It's a tourist who comes to see all the colored leaves in the fall! New Hampshire is one New England state that attracts peepers by the thousands in autumn.

The town of Hillsborough in southern New Hampshire is the birthplace of our fourteenth president, Franklin Pierce.

New Hampshire is the forty-first largest state in population and has about 1.2 million people. Manchester is the largest city and has about 103,000 people. Concord, the state capital, has only about 30,000.

- New Hampshire, in its early days, was known for producing paper and **textiles,** and generating electricity by damming up rivers.
- The Appalachian Mountains, which go as far south as Alabama, and as far north as Quebec, Canada, are very old. Old mountain chains are lower and more rounded.
- Mountains, like beaches, get worn away by erosion. Water drips into the cracks in rocks, all over the mountain. As water freezes, it expands and cracks the rock apart, wearing away a little more every year.
- **textiles:** Woven or knit cloth, made out of any materials (usually cotton or wool).

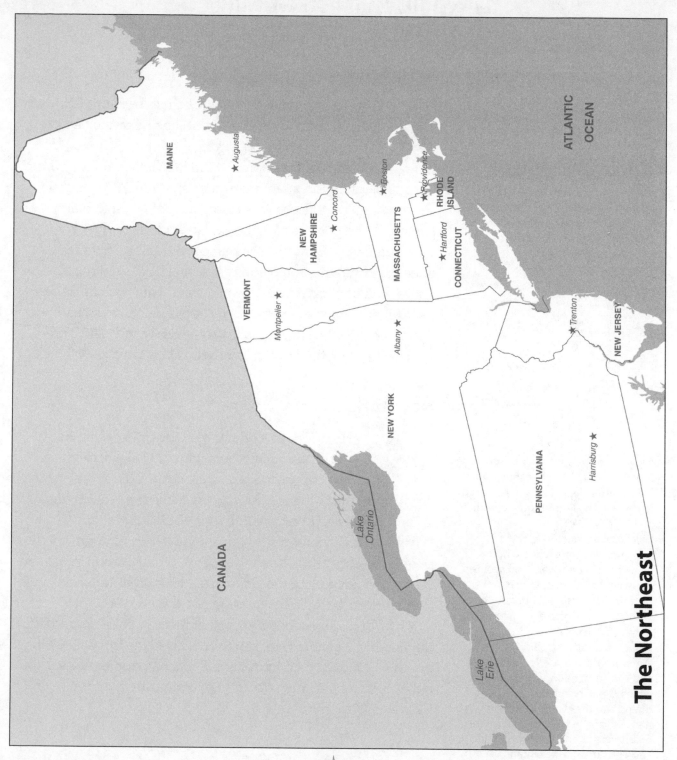

MAINE

★ Augusta

VERMONT

NEW HAMPSHIRE

Montpelier ★

Concord ★

Boston ★

MASSACHUSETTS

Providence ★

RHODE ISLAND

★ Hartford

CONNECTICUT

Albany ★

NEW YORK

CANADA

Lake Ontario

Lake Erie

PENNSYLVANIA

Harrisburg ★

Trenton ★

NEW JERSEY

ATLANTIC OCEAN

The Northeast

New Jersey

- Island Beach is a barrier island. It forms a kind of barrier between the ocean and the mainland. Every big storm changes an island like this. Some storms wash sand away, making it smaller. Others move sand onto the island from somewhere else, making it bigger or even joining it to the coast.

New Jersey has lots of suburbs for New York City and Philadelphia. New Jersey also has its own cities like Newark and Atlantic City.

Visit the Morristown National Historical Park where George Washington spent the winter of 1779–1780 with the Continental Army. There was also plenty of wood to build a camp, and he could watch the British soldiers in New York.

Island Beach State Park is part of the Jersey Shore. See dunes, a nature center, a sandy beach, shells, and a lighthouse. You can drive partway out—then walk or dune buggy!

New Jersey has the ninth largest population, with just under 8.2 million people. Newark is the largest city, with 268,000 people. Trenton, the capital, has only a little over 84,000.

New York

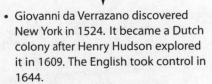

- Giovanni da Verrazano discovered New York in 1524. It became a Dutch colony after Henry Hudson explored it in 1609. The English took control in 1644.
- Glacial lakes, like those in the Adirondacks, were made when a glacier pushed forward and scoured away land with rocks frozen into the bottom—like using sandpaper on wax. When the glacier melted, it left behind "finger" lakes.
- What makes the Niagara Falls fall? Water from the Superior, Michigan, and Huron lakes ends up in Lake Erie, which is much smaller. Lake Erie drains into the Niagara River, which flows northwest over the falls—the height of a twenty-story building!—and ends up in Lake Ontario.

New York has one of the biggest cities in the world, and some amazing natural wonders, too. You can visit Adirondack Park, a giant area of 2,800 lakes, and Niagara Falls, a waterfall area so big and loud that you won't be able to hear people talk!

New York City offers a million things to do. You can watch people trading stocks at the New York Stock Exchange, or see plenty of dinosaurs at the American Museum of Natural History. Even walking down the street is an adventure!

New York is the second largest state in population and has about 18.2 million people. New York City is the largest city in the United States, with more than 8 million people. Albany, the state's capital, has only about one eighty-fifth the population of New York City.

Pennsylvania

 This state's northwest corner is actually on Lake Erie, and the peninsula there has a big park— 3,200 acres. Pennsylvania also has a Little League Baseball Museum and two large cities, Pittsburgh and Philadelphia.

The Little League Museum is in Williamsport. You can video your swing and then watch it, and look at the uniforms of some big-league players who played Little League first.

The Declaration of Independence was written during Continental Congress, held in Philadelphia in 1776. You can also visit the Liberty Bell, from the days of Colonial America.

Pennsylvania is the fifth most populated state, with almost 12 million people. Harrisburg is the capital, but Philadelphia is by far the largest city with about 1.4 million people.

- The land that is now Pennsylvania came under British rule beginning in 1664. The first governor was a Quaker, William Penn, in 1681.
- Philadelphia was the nation's capital until 1800.

Rhode Island

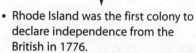 Rhode Island is the smallest state in the United States. It looks as though the ocean took a big, jagged bite out of its east/southeast side—that's Narragansett Bay.

Near the town of Portsmouth is a place called Green Animals. It's a **topiary** garden with trees and shrubs that have been trained and clipped to look like giant animals. Look for the camel, goat, and giraffe. There are beautiful flowers, too.

Newport, closer to the tip of Narragansett Bay, is known for its huge mansions and pleasant wharf area. It's a resort town in the grandest style.

Rhode Island is the forty-third largest state in population and has only about 991,000 people. Providence, the capital and largest city, has about 151,000 people.

- Rhode Island was the first colony to declare independence from the British in 1776.
- Rhode Island is on the Atlantic Flyway, one of the three biggest bird migration routes in the United States. (The other two are the Mississippi River Flyway and the Pacific Flyway.) Birds use these routes to keep from getting lost when migrating from north to south and south to north. They also use the Atlantic Flyway for "speed boosts." When the wind is going the right way, it gives them a push on their migration.
- *topiary:* Plants (like bushes and trees) trimmed to make unusual shapes.

Vermont

- If your sweet tooth kicks in, you can visit Ben and Jerry's Ice Cream factory near Waterbury, Vermont. Not only do you get to see them making the ice cream, you get samples, too!
- How did the Great Lakes form? First glaciers scooped out the land. Then rain, plus the glaciers melting, made the lakes. Lake Champlain got here just that way, too.

This New England state has the Green Mountains (part of the Appalachian Chain), lots of rolling hills and lakes, part of huge Lake Champlain, and a floating bridge that you can drive over. It is also the birthplace of President Calvin Coolidge.

Lake Champlain is such a huge lake that, at one point, people tried to get it called a Great Lake. No deal—it's not *that* big! But Vermont has many nice state parks on its shores.

The floating bridge in the city of Brookfield is weird! You can also walk across it if you're too nervous to drive.

Vermont is the forty-eighth largest state in population and has only 594,000 people. Burlington is the largest city and has a little over 38,000 people, and Montpelier, the capital, has just under 8,000.

QUICK QUIZ

Capitals Quiz

Name the four state capitals that were named after presidents of the United States.

Answer: Madison (Wisconsin), Lincoln (Nebraska), Jackson (Mississippi), and Jefferson City (Missouri)

Glossary

badlands: Region of high hills with many colorful rock layers and jagged edges.

barrier island: An island close to the shore that comes between the ocean and the land. There are lots of them along the Atlantic coast, especially in North Carolina, South Carolina, and Georgia. They are usually just sandbars, and so they sometimes move when there's a big hurricane. Small ones can even get completely washed away.

botany: The science and study of plants and plant life. If you study botany, you'll learn why apple trees grow in the north, orange trees grow in the south, and cacti grow in the desert.

butte: A steep and isolated hill.

caricature: An exaggerated version of something, done in a funny way. Good caricatures usually pick one feature that really stands out, and then make it bigger. Be careful, though! You could do a good caricature of someone with big ears, or a big nose, but they might not like it. If you can, pick a really nice feature, and concentrate on that.

circulation: The movement of your blood around your body. Circulation involves your heart, your lungs, your blood vessels, and more.

decomposed: Broken down to the most basic parts or elements. Fruits and vegetables that have started to rot are just starting to decompose.

discreetly: Quietly, without drawing attention. If you need to sneeze at the dinner table, it's polite to discreetly turn your head and cover your mouth, and not make a big scene sneezing on everyone else's plate.

dormant: Temporarily or seemingly inactive. Dormant volcanoes erupt rarely; extinct ones don't erupt at all.

emu: A flightless bird, related to (but smaller than) the ostrich. Like ostriches, emus are originally from Australia.

equator: The central "belt" around the fattest part of our planet, the middle. It's not a real belt or a real line, but it divides the earth into the northern and southern hemispheres.

erode: To slowly wear, or wash away. Hurricanes and ocean storms have eroded many beaches, due to strong winds and rough seas.

eructation: A fancy word for burping. Just try this word out on your family!

esophagus: The tube that leads between your mouth and your stomach.

fault: A crack between two slabs of rock in the earth's crust. These cracks and fractures are weak spots where earthquakes are most likely to occur.

fictitious: Artificial or imagined, not true (like a fiction novel instead of a nonfiction history book).

glacier: A large, slow-moving body of ice that either comes down from mountains, or spreads outward. Currently, most glaciers are in the polar regions, around the North and South poles.

key: A low island or reef.

latitude: A number that tells you where you are between the equator (latitude 0°) and either the North or South poles (latitude 90°). For example, Minneapolis, Minnesota, is at 45° latitude, exactly halfway between the equator and the North Pole.

local: Related to a specific and limited area; not general or widespread.

mesa: A steep and isolated hill or mountain, like a butte, but especially flat on top. The word "mesa" is Spanish for "table."

peninsula: An area of land that is surrounded by water on three sides.

populated: Refers to the number of people in an area. Cities are heavily populated, which means that many people live and work there. Do you think rural areas are heavily populated?

port city: A city on an ocean, large lake, or river, with big docks, buoys, and all the equipment that large ships need to load and unload their cargo. Many very old and well-known cities around the world are located on the water because that's where international trading ships landed.

quarry: A huge hole dug into the ground to get out large amounts of rock.

raptor: A hunting bird with claws for grabbing prey.

refinery: The building and equipment used to get the impurities out of something. Oil, sugar, and metal need to be processed in a refinery before they can be used.

respiratory: Having to do with the body's breathing system.

rural: Relating to open spaces, as in the country. Rural areas are usually very far from cities. The houses are usually far apart, and you may see a lot of farms.

secede: For one thing to separate itself from a group or organization. During the Civil War, several states seceded from the United States (the Union) to form their own group (the Confederacy).

segregation: Forced separation. The Civil Rights movement had many goals, but one was to end the forced separation of black and white people in schools, restaurants, churches, and buses—everywhere!

textiles: Woven or knit cloth, made out of any materials (usually cotton or wool).

topiary: Plants (like bushes and trees) trimmed to make unusual shapes.

trachea: Your windpipe, the tube where the air goes back and forth to your lungs.

transcontinental: Across the continent. The prefix "trans" usually means across or beyond.

utopia: An imaginary place, often with ideal and perfect laws and government.

PUZZLE ANSWERS

page vi • Word Search

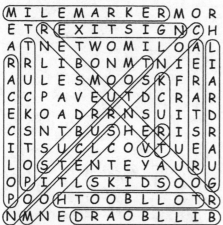

Extra letters spell: More than two million miles of paved roads in this country alone!

page viii • MPG

Sealed With A Kiss

page 2 • MPG

Today's special is a tomato sandwich.

Put bacon and lettuce on mine.

Bacon, Lettuce, & Tomato

page 3 • Pickup Truck

Why are sleepy people like automobile wheels?

B E C A U S E
T H E Y
A R E
T I R E D !

page 5 • A Short Trip

TRAVEL

1. RAVEL   omit "T"

2. REVAL   switch "A" and "E"

3. RELAV   switch "L" and "V"

4. RELAX   change "V" to "X"

page 7 • Let's Get Packing

1. Call Kelly Short for directions to State park.

2. Buy sun block and bug spray.

3. Check the flashlight batteries.

4. Fill water bottles, make snacks, and get chocolate!

5. Pack ponchos and extra socks.

6. Find binoculars and bird books.

PUZZLE ANSWERS

page 11 • State Your Name

WEDLAAER	DELAWARE
IOLRAFNCAI	CALIFORNIA
FAIRDLO	FLORIDA
DINOALERDHS	RHODE ISLAND
UTDSOAHTAOK	SOUTH DAKOTA
ZANIROA	ARIZONA
MAAABLA	ALABAMA
WIAIHA	HAWAII
NOTEVRM	VERMONT
SLAAAK	ALASKA
YCEKKUTN	KENTUCKY
ICMNIHGA	MICHIGAN

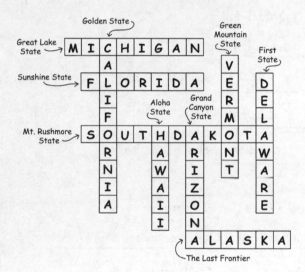

Great Lake State → **MICHIGAN**
Golden State → C A L I F O R N I A
Sunshine State → **FLORIDA**
Aloha State
Grand Canyon State
Mt. Rushmore State → **SOUTH DAKOTA**
Green Mountain State → **VERMONT**
First State → **DELAWARE**
ALASKA ← The Last Frontier

page 15 • Trashmobile

page 16 • Word Search

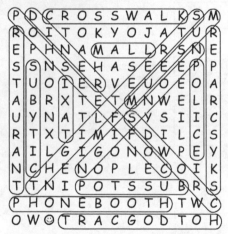

Extra letters spell: Tokyo, Japan has over twenty six million people in it. Wow!

PUZZLE ANSWERS

page 19 • CUL8R

US4EVR
US Forever

Patriotic Person

XQZME
Excuse Me

Polite Person

SK8RS
Skaters

Skating Family

TOTDOC
Tot Doc

Pediatrician

I4GOT
I Forgot

Bad Memory

HRDDRV
Hard Drive

Computer Person

H82W8
Hate To Wait

Impatient Person

IMFUNE
I'm Funny

Comedian

5KIDZ
5 Kids

Big Family

10SNE1
Tennis Anyone?

Looking For
Tennis Partner

W8NC
Wait And See

Patient Person

PB4UGO
Pee Before You Go

Mom's Reminder

page 22• MPG

Save Our Ship

page 26• MPG

Mind Your Own Business

page 27 • On the Road

page 28• MPG

Pick Your Own

PUZZLE ANSWERS

page 29 • **Family Album**

page 30 • **Word Search**

Extra letters spell:
She sells seashells by the seashore.

page 33 • **Word Search**

Extra letters spell: It is twenty-nine
thousand and twenty-eight feet tall.

page 34 • **MPG**

Unidentified Flying Object

PUZZLE ANSWERS

page 35 • **Beep Beep**

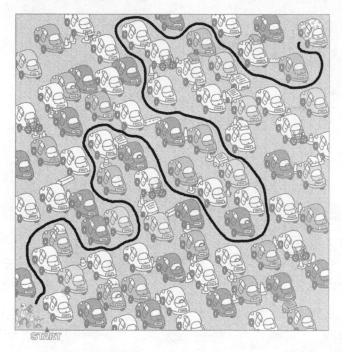

page 68 • **MPG**

Laugh Out Loud

page 69 • **Pit Stop**

page 71 • **Batty Billboard**

TRADER BOB'S BIG **SHOE SALE** THIS INCREDIBLY SUPER SALE WILL ONLY LAST A VERY SHORT TIME. SHOP FOR SHOES — NOW!

PUZZLE ANSWERS

page 72 • **MPG**

> *HURRY! Mail this right away!*
>
> *Don't wait!*

<u>A</u>s <u>S</u>oon <u>A</u>s <u>P</u>ossible

page 74 • **Who Parked Where?**

	vehicle	state	color
man with dog	van	Ohio	blue
twin sisters	truck	Maine	silver
family	sports car	New York	red

page 76 • **Word Search**

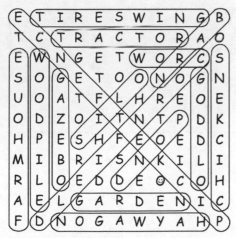

Extra letters spell:
To get to the other side!

page 77 • **Parking Lot**

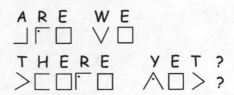

page 97 • **Pretty Postcards**

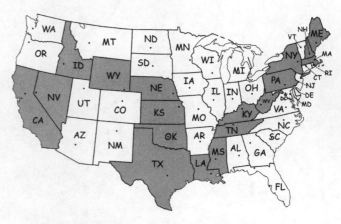

page 106 • **Heading Home**

START			
SEA	SHELL	FISH	HOOK
HORSE	BACK	HAND	BALL
FLY	YARD	OUT	GAME
PAPER	STICK	BREAK	DOWN
BACK	FIRE	FAST	TOWN FINISH

page 112 • **Cross-Country Chuckles**

What did *DELAWARE (Dela wear)* ?
She wore her *NEW JERSEY* !

What did *TENNESSEE (Tennes see)*?
She saw what *ARKANSAS (Arkan saw)* !

What did *IDAHO (Ida hoe)* ?
She hoed her *MARYLAND (merry land)* !

Index

Index

About the Authors

Erik began college at Harvard University, left to take time off, and is now working toward a B.S. in Biological Science Writing at the University of Minnesota. He lives in the Minneapolis area and works part-time at a bookstore.

Jeanne is a literary agent, the author of *Why Can't You Tickle Yourself?*, published by W.H. Freeman for younger readers, and eight books for adult readers. She also lives in the Minneapolis area.

The Everything® KIDS' Series!

Packed with tons of information, activities, and puzzles, the Everything® Kids' books are perennial bestsellers that keep kids active and engaged.

Each book is $7.95, two-color, 8" x 9¼", and 144 –176 pages.

The Everything® Kids'
Cookbook, 2nd Ed.
ISBN 10: 1-59869-592-4

The Everything® Kids' Dragons
Puzzle and Activity Book
ISBN 10: 1-59869-623-8

The Everything® Kids'
Geography Book
ISBN 10: 1-59869-683-1

The Everything® Kids' Hanukkah
Puzzle and Activity Book
ISBN 10: 1-59869-788-9

The Everything® Kids' Money
Book, 2nd Ed.
ISBN 10: 1-59869-784-6

The Everything® Kids' Mummies,
Pharaohs, and Pyramids Puzzle
and Activity Book
ISBN 10: 1-59869-797-8

The Everything® Kids'
Spelling Book
ISBN 10: 1-59869-754-4

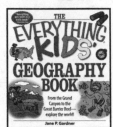

A silly, goofy, and undeniably icky addition to
the Everything® Kids' series . . .

The Everything® Kids'
GROSS
Series

Chock-full of sickening entertainment for hours of disgusting fun.

The Everything® Kids'
Gross Cookbook
1-59869-324-7, $7.95

The Everything® Kids' Gross
Hidden Pictures Book
1-59337-615-4, $7.95

The Everything® Kids'
Gross Jokes Book
1-59337-448-8, $7.95

The Everything® Kids'
Gross Mazes Book
1-59337-616-2, $7.95

The Everything® Kids' Gross
Puzzle & Activity Book
1-59337-447-X, $7.95

Other Everything® Kids' Titles Available

The Everything® Kids' Animal Puzzle & Activity Book
1-59337-305-8

The Everything® Kids' Astronomy Book
1-59869-544-4

The Everything® Kids' Baseball Book, 5th Ed.
1-59869-487-1

The Everything® Kids' Bible Trivia Book
1-59337-031-8

The Everything® Kids' Bugs Book
1-58062-892-3

The Everything® Kids' Cars and Trucks
Puzzle and Activity Book
1-59337-703-7

The Everything® Kids' Christmas Puzzle
& Activity Book
1-58062-965-2

The Everything® Kids' Connect the Dots Puzzle and Activity
Book
1-59869-647-5

The Everything® Kids' Crazy Puzzles Book
1-59337-361-9

The Everything® Kids' Dinosaurs Book
1-59337-360-0

The Everything® Kids' Environment Book
1-59869-670-X

The Everything® Kids' Fairies Puzzle and Activity Book
1-59869-394-8

The Everything® Kids' First Spanish Puzzle and
Activity Book
1-59337-717-7

The Everything® Kids' Football Book
1-59869-565-7

The Everything® Kids' Halloween Puzzle &
Activity Book
1-58062-959-8

The Everything® Kids' Hidden Pictures Book
1-59337-128-4

The Everything® Kids' Horses Book
1-59337-608-1

The Everything® Kids' Joke Book
1-58062-686-6

The Everything® Kids' Knock Knock Book
1-59337-127-6

The Everything® Kids' Learning French Book
1-59869-543-6

The Everything® Kids' Learning Spanish Book
1-59337-716-9

The Everything® Kids' Magical Science Experiments Book
1-59869-426-X

The Everything® Kids' Math Puzzles Book
1-58062-773-0

The Everything® Kids' Mazes Book
1-58062-558-4

The Everything® Kids' Nature Book
1-58062-684-X

The Everything® Kids' Pirates Puzzle and Activity Book
1-59337-607-3

The Everything® Kids' Presidents Book
1-59869-262-3

The Everything® Kids' Princess Puzzle and Activity Book
1-59337-704-5

The Everything® Kids' Puzzle Book
1-58062-687-4

The Everything® Kids' Racecars Puzzle and Activity Book
1-59869-243-7

The Everything® Kids' Riddles & Brain Teasers Book
1-59337-036-9

The Everything® Kids' Science Experiments Book
1-58062-557-6

The Everything® Kids' Sharks Book
1-59337-304-X

The Everything® Kids' Soccer Book
1-58062-642-4

The Everything® Kids' Spies Puzzle and Activity Book
1-59869-409-X

The Everything® Kids' States Book
1-59869-263-1

The Everything® Kids' Travel Activity Book
1-58062-641-6

The Everything® Kids' Word Search Puzzle and Activity
Book
1-59869-545-2

All titles are $6.95 or $7.95 unless otherwise noted.

Available wherever books are sold!
To order, call 800-258-0929, or visit us at *www.adamsmedia.com*
Everything® and everything.com® are registered trademarks of F+W Publications, Inc.
Prices subject to change without notice.